Contemporary
ART
GLASS

Also by Ray and Lee Grover

• ART GLASS NOUVEAU
• CARVED & DECORATED EUROPEAN ART GLASS

Contemporary
ART
GLASS

BY RAY AND LEE GROVER

CROWN PUBLISHERS, INC., NEW YORK

Inquiries should be addressed to
Crown Publishers, Inc., 419 Park Avenue South,
New York, N.Y. 10016.

Printed in the United States of America
Published simultaneously in Canada
by General Publishing Company Limited

Designed by Shari de Miskey

Library of Congress Cataloging in Publication Data

Grover, Ray.
    Contemporary art glass.

    Bibliography: p.
    Includes index.
    1. Glassware.   2. Artists—Biography.
I. Grover, Lee, joint author.   II. Title.
NK5110.G72   748.2′9′22   75-2046
ISBN 0-517-51628-4

Ray and Lee Grover
to our
Children and Grandchildren

Sally–Jerry Dubrow   Donna–Mike Holland   Joyce–Barry Gerstein

Robert Philip, 1957   Ted, 1963   David Joseph, 1967

John Martin, 1958   Betsy Lee, 1966   Daniel Martin, 1969

Jane Elizabeth, 1961   Michael Philip, 1973

Carolyn Sue, 1962

CONTENTS

ACKNOWLEDGMENTS

It has been a rewarding experience to write this book. We have been fortunate to be able to come into personal contact with all the artists whose glass masterpieces are here portrayed. Glass artists dwell in many countries today, and our travels were therefore extensive. They all have their own lives as individuals and as great artists, so our interviews were varied and interesting. They are, as a group, among the most vital and talented people we ever encountered. They shared their time and knowledge with us, and we sincerely thank them all.

In addition to the glass artists in each country, we met many other people who are part of the glass scene and who helped us gather the material we required: officials of various governments; the directors and owners of many glass companies; factory personnel; glassblowers, and other skilled people who assisted us in various ways. It has been astounding to see the far-reaching effects on everyone who is touched by the glass story, as it lives and breathes today.

For the cooperation that made CONTEMPORARY ART GLASS possible, we particularly wish to express our appreciation to the following:

CZECHOSLOVAKIA:

>Michael Gelvar, Curator, Museum of Glass, Novy Bor
>Stefan Hronsky, Glassexport, Liberec
>Frank Janda, President, Superlux Ltd., New York
>Jindrich Kadlec, Glassexport, Liberec
>Ladislav Mlejnek, Director, Glassexport, Liberec
>Jiri Neubauer, Institute of Interior and Fashion Design, Prague
>Marie Simerdova, Glassexport, Liberec

Ralph R. Stern, Vice-President, Superlux Ltd., New York
Ivo Vesely, Rapid Co.

DENMARK:

Hans Hartman Berg, Kastrup-Holmegaard Glass, Copenhagen

ENGLAND:

J. Michael Dumeresque, Berkswell, Warwickshire
Diana Rivett, The Crafts Centre of Great Britain, London
Irene M. Stevens, Stourbridge
Rosalind Sutton, The Crafts Centre of Great Britain, London
Helen Monro Turner, Juniper Green, Scotland

FRANCE:

Jacques Daum, President, Cristallerie de Nancy, Nancy
Pierre De Cherisey, Cristallerie Daum, Paris

FINLAND:

Goran Anderson, Nuutajarvi Lasi Oy.
H.O. Gummerus, Director General, Finnish Society of Crafts and Design,
   Helsinki
Miss Peltola, Office of Consulate General of Finland, New York
Jorma Simojoki, Riihimaen Lasi Oy.
Tatu Tuohikorpi, Foreign Office of Finland, Helsinki
Mrs. Valkama, Office of Consulate General of Finalnd, New York
Lusa and Erkki Vesanto, Iittala
Maaria Wirkkala, Helsinki
Rut and Tapio Wirkkala, Helsinki
Sami Wirkkala, Helsinki

ITALY:

Flavio Barbini
Mr. and Mrs. Ludovico Diaz De Santillana, Murano, Venice
Pier Andrea Molon, Salviati, Venice
Oceania Barbini Moretti
Sandra Ruffini, Murano, Venice
Renzo Tedeschi, Director, Salviati, Venice

NORWAY:

Jens W. Berg, General Manager, Hadeland Glasverk, Jevnaker
Mrs. Brita Florelius, Hadeland Glassverk, Jevnaker
Bernhard Matheson, Director Organesasjoven Plus, Frederikstad
General B. Frederik Motzfeldt, Oslo

SWEDEN:

Johan Beyer, President, Orrefors Glassworks
Ingvai Carlsson, Pukebergs Glassworks
Mrs. Ann Margaret Franzon, Boda Glassworks
Veine Franzen, Afors Glassworks
Carl Gronberg, Orrefors Glassworks
Ann-Beate Jonsson, Antikvorie Vid, Smalands Museum, Vaxjo
Miss Helga Rotter, Kosta Glassworks
Jan-Eric Stromberg, Stromberg Huttan

UNITED STATES:

Helen and Marvin Fox, Cleveland, Ohio
Mary Martin Kraus, Larchmont, New York
James Kux, Naples, Florida
Libby Labino, Grand Rapids, Ohio
Paul N. Perrot, Assistant Secretary for Museum Programs, The Smithsonian Institution, Washington, D.C.
Doris Reeder, Naples, Florida
Miss Jane S. Shadel, Assistant Curator of American Glass, The Corning Museum of Glass, Corning, New York
Kenneth M. Wilson, Director of Collections and Preservation, Greenfield Village, Henry Ford Museum, Dearborn, Michigan

WEST GERMANY:

Alfons Eisch, Frauenau
Erich Eisch, Frauenau
Gretel Eisch, Frauenau
N. Kainz, Frauenau
Professor Konrad Habermeier, Schwab. Gmund
Bernhard Schagemann, Zwiesel
Alois Streichsbier, Gral-Glashutte, Durnau

FOREWORD

In our extensive travels to do the research for this book, and to collect the individual pieces that are shown here, we soon became aware that modern art glass has developed by two different routes:

In Europe, for example, glass artists are often sponsored by the factories, but the artists are not so stifled by industrialization as they once were. Although these artists and designers may, for the most part, achieve their ends through the use of the factory glassblower, they also have time to exploit the possibilities of many technical approaches and styles, and individual artists have their own workshops for the creations that begin on their sketch desks. Moreover, not only do many European factories have a rich historical background that goes back hundreds of years; they are forward-looking firms willing to exploit individual ideas and techniques and make them available internationally. The glass artists themselves benefit from this "partnership," for they are able to make their involvement with glass a lifetime work, and such continuity of endeavor is both the inspiration and lifeblood of successful experimentation. With today's ease of distribution and transportation, their work is given wide exposure at annual international fairs not only in Europe and the United States but also in the Orient.

It should also be pointed out that the European glass artist at no time leaves his ideas to be worked over by the glassblowers. For all practical purposes, he stays right with an idea until the glass finally goes into the annealing oven for cooling and tempering. The master glassblower is the physical arm of the artist, who is at all times the director-general of his own creation.

In the United States, on the other hand, modern art glass has come into its own through a quite different approach. Prior to 1962 there were only a few artists working with free-blown glass. Then, through the major efforts of Harvey Littleton,

Dominick Labino, the Toledo Museum and its director, Otto Wittmann, two glass seminars were instituted and glassblowing in this country was reestablished as an important creative art. The first workshop came into being through a grant from the University of Wisconsin, where Littleton was teaching. Since that time many American Universities have set up complete courses and facilities for the rising American group of glass artists. Many of these artists are teachers who have finally become prolific in their own right, building their own kilns, designing and bringing to personal fruition their own creations. This group of young, exciting artists are building the future of glass in this country, and their influence is widespread.

The biographical information given herein was supplied almost entirely by the glass artists themselves, and therefore it varies noticeably in length and the amount of detail, according to their individual preferences. In the case of foreign glassmen, the biographies differ somewhat in style depending on their fluency in English.

All the photography in this book was done by us, and every piece is in our personal collection.

The height of the glass objects is shown only in inches; no diameters or widths are given. Measurements, for practicality, are to the nearest one-quarter inch.

WILLIAM JOSEPH BERNSTEIN

Born Newark, New Jersey, December 3, 1945

Bernstein
1971

With an early interest in science and art, Bernstein left the public schools in Elizabeth and transferred to the Arts High School in Newark, from which he was graduated in 1963. He entered the University of Wisconsin, but in only a few months he found that he had little in common with the academic world and he left for New York to work in a film studio, as well as attend night classes in film at City College. February 1965 found him at the Philadelphia College of Art, where he majored in ceramics until, in his senior year, he became involved in glassblowing when a shop of limited resources was set up.

Following his graduation in 1968, he married Katherine Schachter, a graduate student in sculpture. Shortly thereafter, they entered the University of Wisconsin for graduate work in glass, but after a week of house-hunting Bernstein received an offer to become Craftsman in Residence at Penland School of Crafts, Penland, North Carolina, and they moved to their current base of operations in western North Carolina.

With the arrival of their son, Joshua Emil, in October 1969, they found a log cabin in Celo Community, a land cooperative near Penland, and in January 1971 converted an old dairy barn into a glass and ceramic studio, now known as The

1

Southtoe River Glass and Earth Works, where original, and frequently organic-styled, glass are deftly produced.

SHOWS:

"Alumni Show of the '60s," Philadelphia College of Art, 1971

Annual Sculpture Show of the Southeast Region, Hon. Mention

"Appalachian Corridors," Charleston, West Virginia, seventeen-state show of the Appalachian Region, 1970. Award of Merit $400

"Art in Other Media," Rockford Art Association, Rockford, Illinois, 1970

"Fiber and Glass," Ithaca College, Museum of Art, Ithaca, New York, 1970

Gallery of Contemporary Arts, Winston-Salem, North Carolina, 1969

"North Carolina Craftsmen," North Carolina Museum of Art, Raleigh, North Carolina, 1971

"Piedmont Craftsmen Show," Mint Museum of Art, Charlotte, North Carolina, 1969, 1970

Two-year traveling show, based on national competition

"Young Americans," American Crafts Council, New York

1. William Bernstein, United States. 12½". Signed "Bernstein, 1968"

2. William Bernstein, United States. 6½". Signed "Bernstein"

3. William Bernstein, United States. 10½". Signed "Bernstein, 1970"

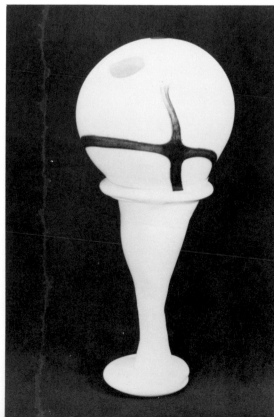

4. William Bernstein, United States. 9¾″. Signed "Bernstein, 1970"

5. William Bernstein, United States. 4¾″. Signed "Bernstein, 1970"

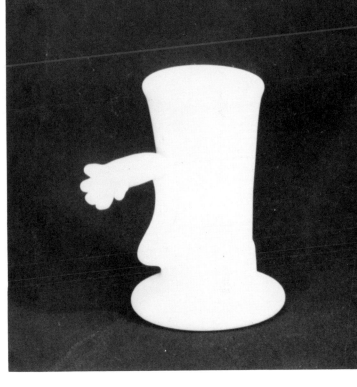

6–7.
William Bernstein, United States. *(Left)* 6″. Signed "Bernstein." *(Right)* 6¾″. Signed "Bernstein"

BOB BINIARZ

First a potter, then an artist working in the challenging field of glass, Biniarz is very conscious of strong forms and fantasy colors. Reminders of the art nouveau period are occasionally evident in some of his pieces, particularly in the swirls and flowerlike lines embodied in his vases. We notice here a strong personal expression, which is to be seen in the work of so many of the younger artists on the scene today, and this in fact is one of the necessary requisites for future important recognition. His work currently may be seen at The Galeria de Sol, Montecito, California, and The Phoenix, Big Sur, California. (See Color Plate 4.)

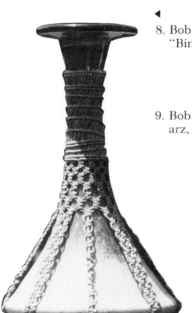

◄

8. Bob Biniarz, United States. 11¼". Signed "Biniarz, '72."

9. Bob Biniarz, United States. 9¼". Signed "Biniarz, '72."

4

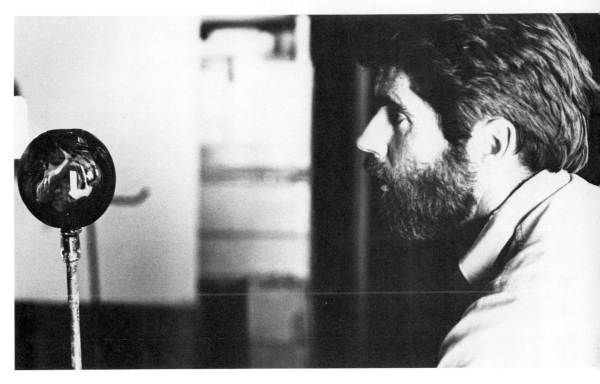

MICHAEL BOYLEN

Born in Janesville, Wisconsin, 1935

After graduating with an A.B. degree from Yale University, and an M.A. in American history from the University of Wisconsin, Boylen studied pottery with Franz Wildenhain at the School for American Craftsmen, and then commenced blowing glass as a graduate student of Harvey Littleton at the University of Wisconsin in 1963. In 1964, he set up the first glass workshop at the Haystack School of Crafts, as well as teaching there, and subsequently at the Penland School of Crafts in Penland, North Carolina.

In 1965, Boylen received a grant for glassblowing from the Louis Comfort Tiffany Foundation. The following year, after a short stint of teaching at the Cleveland Institute of Art, he moved to Vermont. There, he and his wife Claire Van Vliet, a graphic artist, maintain their own studios, teaching part time at various art schools and colleges. Working in his small barn studio with two sixty-pound day tanks, a crucible furnace, and glory hole, he has concentrated on the development and refinement of a technique for building up internal forms in multiple layers and divisions of glass and color. As can be seen in Illustrations 10 through 13 and Color Plate 1, his extreme sensitivity and control are not accidental but the mark of an accomplished artist.

Since 1971, when he toured European glass factories and schools, Boylen has stressed more irregularity of shape and evidenced an interest in the characteristics of the Art Nouveau period. His work is well represented in notable public collections.

Beginning with his earliest student work in 1964, we find his pieces usually marked with a full signature, although some small works made before 1971 have only the initials M.B. Dates frequently occur, and in 1971 there was a consecutive numbering of pieces.

ONE-MAN EXHIBITIONS:
America House, Birmingham, Michigan, 1968
Benson Gallery, Bridgehampton, New York, 1969, 1971
Dartmouth College, Hanover, New Hampshire, 1968
Design Corner, Cleveland, Ohio, 1968, 1971
Helen Winnemore Gallery, Columbus, Ohio, 1971
The Print Club, Philadelphia, 1969
The Works Gallery, Philadelphia, 1970, 1971

INVITATIONAL GROUP EXHIBITIONS:
Arts and Science Center, Nashua, New Hampshire, 1971
Dallas Museum of Fine Arts, 1967
De Cordova and Dana Museum and Park, Lincoln, Massachusetts, 1958, 1970
Edinburgh College of Art, Edinburgh, Scotland, 1965–66
Hunterdon Art Center, Clinton, New Jersey, 1969
Museum West, San Francisco, 1965
Ontario Craft Foundation, Sheridan College, Toronto and Montreal, 1970
Royal College of Art, London, 1965–66
Society of Arts and Crafts, Boston, 1965
Stratton Arts Festival, 1970, 1971
University of Wisconsin Group, 1965–66

NATIONAL AND REGIONAL JURIED EXHIBITIONS:
Brockton Art Center, Brockton, Massachusetts, 1972
Cleveland Museum of Art, 44th May Show, 1966
"Crafts 1970," Institute of Contemporary Art, Boston
"Craftsmen, U.S.A.," North Central Region, 1966
Delaware Art Center, Wilmington, 1971
Miami National Ceramic Exhibition, 1965
Smithsonian Institution Traveling Exhibition, 1968/9
Southern Tier Crafts Show, Corning Museum of Glass, Corning, New York, 1971, 1972
Syracuse (New York) Ceramic National, 1964, 1968
Toledo Glass Nationals, 1966, 1968

PUBLIC COLLECTIONS:
Bennington (Vermont) Museum

Cleveland Museum of Art, Cleveland, Ohio
Corning Museum of Glass, Corning, New York
Dartmouth College, Hanover, New Hampshire
Delaware Art Museum, Wilmington
Fleming Museum, University of Vermont, Burlington
Milwaukee Art Center, Milwaukee, Wisconsin
University of Wisconsin, Madison

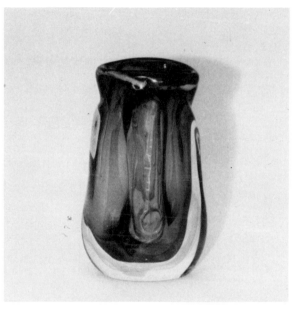

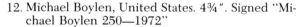

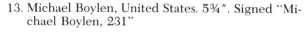

10. Michael Boylen, United States. 5″. Signed "Michael Boylen, 173"

11. Michael Boylen, United States. 6″. Signed "Michael Boylen 380—1972"

12. Michael Boylen, United States. 4¾″. Signed "Michael Boylen 250—1972"

13. Michael Boylen, United States. 5¾″. Signed "Michael Boylen, 231"

Jack Brewer

JACK BREWER

One of the more active Florida glassmen, Jack Brewer became interested in the art field at the age of fourteen under the guidance of Robert Sprague. He received his Bachelor of Arts degree from the University of South Florida, attended the Penland School of Crafts, Penland, North Carolina, and then proceeded to set up a private studio in glass and ceramics in St. Petersburg, Florida. A member of the Florida Craftsman Association, Brewer taught art at the Safety Harbor Junior High School for three years before deciding to spend full time in glass. He is currently in the process of building a studio in the mountains of North Carolina. (See Color Plate 2.)

14.
Jack Brewer, United States. 11¼". Signed "JAK, 1971"

EXHIBITIONS AND AWARDS:

Clearwater Art Show, Florida, first place
Cocoa Beach Art Show, Florida, first place
Contemporary Gallery, St. Petersburg, Florida
Craftique, Jacksonville, Florida
Creative Crafts, Pensacola, Florida
Florida Craftsman Art Show, purchase award
Gallery of Art, Panama City, Florida
Indialantic Art Show, Florida, third place
Jacksonville Art Museum, Jacksonville, Florida
Museum of Fine Arts, St. Petersburg, Florida
The Pot Shop, Largo, Florida
Smithsonian Institution Traveling Show
Toledo Glass Nationals
Trend House Gallery, Tampa, Florida
Up There Gallery, Sarasota, Florida
Winter Haven Art Show, Florida, purchase award

15. Jack Brewer, United States. 11″.
Signed "JAK, 1971"

16. Jack Brewer, United States. 8¾″.
Signed "JAK, 1971"

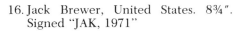

donald carlson

DONALD CARLSON

Located in Pacifica, California, Donald Carlson is not only well grounded in the academic art field but has spent considerable time in furnace design and construction, in the belief that a foundation of good equipment is essential to the production of fine glass. In this respect he is self-taught; he has also developed a personal style through his own experimentation. Precise control and skillful manipulation of the glass in quite simple shapes and forms, with emphasis on surface colors and textures, are what he is known for, although new techniques, followed by a two-month study in Europe in 1970, have given him a fresh outlook.

Carlson received his Bachelor of Science degree in 1967 at San Jose State College; his Bachelor of Arts in 1969 at San Francisco State College, and his Master of Arts degree there in 1972. At present, he is endeavoring to branch out commercially and appeal to the contemporary collector. (See Color Plate 3.)

EXHIBITIONS:

"Designer Craftsman '71," Richmond Art Center, Richmond, California

Glass and Leather Invitational, Fair Tree Gallery of Contemporary Crafts, New York, 1972

"Media '70" and "Media '72," Civic Arts Gallery, Walnut Creek, California

San Francisco Civic Arts Show, 1971

San Francisco Potters' Association Biennial, De Young Museum, San Francisco, 1970

ONE-MAN SHOWS:

Afterimage, Sacramento, California, 1972

Cooperhouse, Santa Cruz, California, 1972

San Francisco State College, 1972

Sign of the Acorn, Wichita, Kansas, 1972

17.
Donald Carlson, United States. 4¾". Signed "Carlson, 1971"

18.
Donald Carlson, United States. 5". Signed "Carlson, 1972"

19.
Donald Carlson, United States. 5½″. Signed
"Carlson, 1972"

20.
Donald Carlson, United States. 5½″. Signed
"Carlson, 1972"

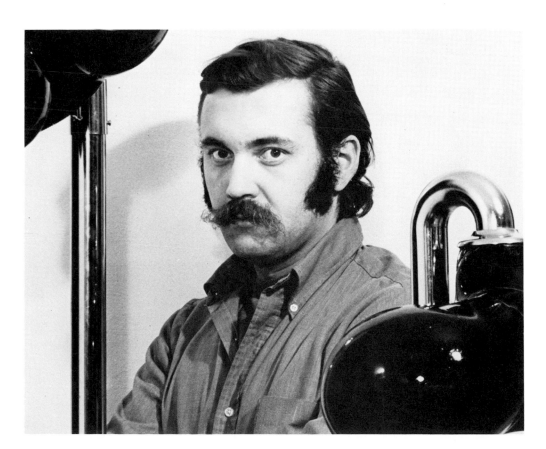

BORIS DUDCHENKO

Born in the Ukraine, May 4, 1943

One of the more prolific glass sculpture artists, Dudchenko has considerable influence in his field today. His first eight years were spent in Hanover, Germany; he came to the United States in 1951.

After receiving a Bachelor of Science degree in art education at Kutztown State College in 1965, and an M.F.A. at the University of Wisconsin in 1967, Dudchenko continued his work under the guidance of several glassmen, including Donald Reitz, N. Wayne Taylor, Abram Schlemowitz, and Harvey Littleton. He became assistant professor in ceramics and glassblowing in 1967 at the Carnegie–Mellon University, Pittsburgh. This has been a continuing association, for his home and private furnaces are in nearby Greensburg, Pennsylvania. His wife, Nancy, whom he married in 1966, is an accomplished and recognized potter in her own right; she works alongside Boris, using her own kilns, on their farm. Both strive to realize their personal creative inspirations in their individual work.

Believing that, even after several thousand years of glass innovations, there are still no limits, Dudchenko endeavors through sculptural glassblowing in conjunction with other materials to create pieces of notable individuality. He stresses individual creativity in his classroom work as well; rather than emphasize his own particular approach to the field, he thinks every successful artist has a specific personal contribution to make. (See Color Plates 5 and 7.)

It would be redundant to list all the over one hundred and more exhibitions and shows the Dudchenkos have been invited to, and the numerous lectures Dudchenko has given in Europe and in the United States. His popularity can be appreciated from the following partial list.

ONE-MAN SHOWS (1966–72):

Arkansas Art Center, Little Rock, Arkansas, 1970

Baum Art School, Allentown, Pennsylvania, 1968

California State College, California, Pennsylvania, 1969

Carlow College, Pittsburgh, Pennsylvania, 1971

Carnegie Institute, Museum of Art, Pittsburgh, Pennsylvania, 1971

Edgewood College of the Sacred Heart, Madison, Wisconsin, 1966

Paine Art Center, Oshkosh, Wisconsin, 1971

Pennsylvania State University, Chambers Gallery, State College, Pennsylvania, 1972

Seton Hill College, Greensburg, Pennsylvania, 1970, 1972

Slippery Rock State College, Slippery Rock, Pennsylvania, 1969

West Virginia University, Creative Arts Center, Morgantown, 1970

COMPETITIVE GROUP EXHIBITIONS:

Ann Arbor Art Festival, Ann Arbor, Michigan, 1970, 1971, 1972

"Appalachian Corridors," I and II, Charleston, West Virginia, 1968, 1970

Associated Artists of Pittsburgh Annual Shows, 58th, 60th, and 62nd, Pittsburgh, Pennsylvania, 1968, 1970, 1972

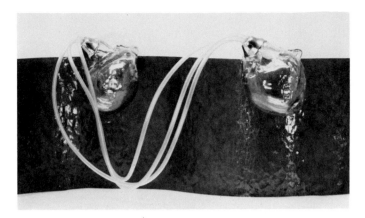

21.
Boris Dudchenko, United States. 15″. Signed
"Boris Dudchenko"

22.
Boris Dudchenko, United States. 16½″. Signed
"Boris Dudchenko"

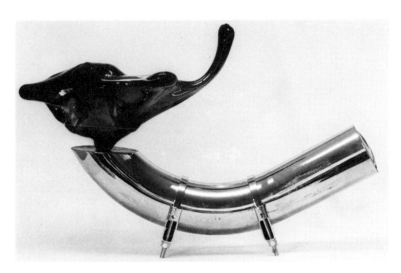

23.
Boris Dudchenko, United States. 17″. Signed
"Boris Dudchenko"

Carnegie–Mellon University Faculty Show, Pittsburgh, 1969, 1970, 1971

Contemporary Gallery of Fine Arts, Dallas, Texas, 1968

Craft Show, 30th Annual, Rockford, Illinois, 1966

Craftsmen's Guild, 24th, 25th, 26th, 27th, 28th Exhibitions, Pittsburgh, Pennsylvania, 1968–72

Erie Summer Festival of the Arts, Exhibition '69, '70, Erie, Pennsylvania

Exposition of Wisconsin Art (53rd Annual), Milwaukee, 1967

"Glass 14th Century B.C. to 1971 A.D.," Jim Kohler Arts Center Glass Invitational, Sheboygan, Wisconsin, 1971

Greater Fall River Art Association, Inc., Fall River, Massachusetts, Annual Show, 1968

Lakefront Festival, Milwaukee, Wisconsin, annually 1968 through 1972

Long Beach Museum of Art Invitational, Long Beach, California, 1971

Madison Artists (27th Annual) Exhibition, Madison, Wisconsin, 1966

"Objects, U.S.A.," The Johnson Wax Collection, Racine, Wisconsin, four-year tour of the United States and Europe

Show (6th Annual) of Drawing, Prints, & Sculptures, Pittsburgh, 1967–68

Society of Sculptors, Annual Exhibition, Pittsburgh, 1970, 1972

Southern Tier Arts and Crafts Annual Shows, Corning, New York, 1968, 1969, 1970

Spring Art Exhibit Invitationals, 3rd, 4th, and 5th Annuals, Pennsylvania State University, Beaver Campus, Monaco, Pennsylvania, 1968, 1969, 1970

Three Rivers Art Festival, Pittsburgh, Pennsylvania, 1968 through 1972

Westmoreland County Museum of Art, 4th, 5th, 6th, and 7th Invitational Regionals of Painting and Sculpture, Greensburg, Pennsylvania, 1968 through 1971

EDRIS ECKHARDT

Born in Cleveland, Ohio, January 28, 1910

One of the outstanding studio artists on the American scene today, Edris Eckhardt is also recognized as one of the foremost teachers of the last forty years, not only in glass but in ceramics as well. From 1927 through 1932 she attended the Cleveland Institute of Art, specializing in sculpture, ceramics, and the handling of various surface glazes. Her teaching experience—commencing with the Cleveland Institute of Art, in ceramics, 1933–60, and including Western Reserve University School of Applied Sciences (ceramics, enamels, and crafts), 1947–58; University of California at Berkeley, where she started the glass department in 1962; Notre Dame College, South Euclid, Ohio, 1966–69—has permanently established her reputation in the academic field. She is also nationally recognized in the ceramic art world.

Her earliest glass experiments, in 1953, centered on rediscovering the methods used by the late-Roman glassmakers in the manufacture of gold glasses, particularly in the effects that could be achieved by laminating gold between sheets of glass. Using the skill and knowledge gained in her studies at the Metropolitan Museum of Art and the Corning Museum of Glass, she not only succeeded in producing gold glass but also discovered how to duplicate the fine reds and blues in the stained glass windows of European cathedrals—in particular, the famous windows of Chartres Cathedral. Closely following her initial work in the glass medium, she received two fellowships from the Guggenheim Foundation, and in 1959 won a Tiffany Foundation Award.

In the 1960s, as her experience in glass increased, she started executing sculptures, many of them with a religious background. Then, not being satisfied with just ceramics or glass, Miss Eckhardt proceeded to combine glass with bronze; personally she considers this marriage one of her major accomplishments.

In our opinion, Edris Eckhardt will undoubtedly be most remembered for her investment casting in glass. Known as the cire perdue, or lost-wax, method of manufacture, this requires a hand-carved wax model, which is then coated with a high-strength ceramic. When this unit is heated, the wax runs out of the ceramic shell, and is subsequently replaced with powdered glass. Upon refiring, the powdered glass

becomes viscous, after which it is slowly cooled in an annealing oven. When the cooling is complete, the ceramic shell is broken off, leaving the final glass sculpture. In the history of glass, very few have succeeded with this type of glass sculpture. One of those who had outstanding success with it was Frederick Carder, head of the Steuben Glass Works from 1903 to 1918. Carder began to experiment with the lost-wax process in the early 1930s, when he was art director of Corning Glass Works, and in subsequent years and during his retirement produced many fine examples. At the present time the Daum factory in France, through a different approach, is making limited editions of this type of sculpture. Miss Eckhardt, however, has received international recognition for her unique pieces in this category. (See Color Plates 6 and 8.)

Edris Eckhardt has sixty-eight pieces of ceramics and glass in forty-five permanent museum collections, and in addition has won fifty-six national and international awards. She has exhibited in five world's fairs, and has made and sold over four thousand pieces of glass since 1953. Her shows and exhibitions read like a directory of the world of contemporary art, but only a few of the major ones in the glass field are listed here.

American Federation of Art, Western States, 1968
Butler Institute of American Art, Youngstown, Ohio, 1957
Cleveland Museum of Art, 1956–57–58
Corning Museum of Glass, Corning, New York, 1959, 1968
Dallas Museum of Art, Dallas, Texas, 1964
Kirk on the Hills, Bloomfield, Michigan, 1955
Lowe Art Museum, University of Miami, 1957–58
Massillon Museum of Art, Massillon, Ohio, 1956
National Religious Art, Birmingham, Michigan, 1964
Sheridan College, Oakville, Ontario, traveling show, 1970
Smithsonian Institution, Washington, D.C.
Syracuse Museum of Art, Syracuse, New York
Toledo Glass National, 1966
Western Hemisphere Exhibition, 1956–57, two-year traveling show
Wichita Museum, Wichita, Kansas

24.
Edris Eckhardt, United States. 12″.
Signed "Edris Eckhardt, 1969"

25.
Edris Eckhardt, United States. 10″.
Signed "Edris Eckhardt"

26.
Edris Eckhardt, United States. 9″.
Signed "Edris Eckhardt, 1967"

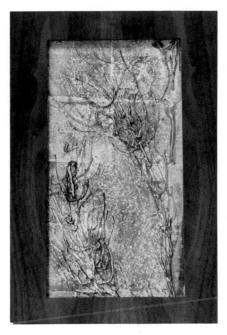

27. Edris Eckhardt, United States. 19½″. Signed "Edris Eckhardt, Winter Dreams of Spring"

28. Edris Eckhardt, United States. 18¼″. Signed "Edris Eckhardt, 1966, Burning Bush"

◄

29. Edris Eckhardt, United States. 13″. Signed "Edris Eckhardt, 1965"

30. Edris Eckhardt, United States. 16″. Signed "1962, Edris"

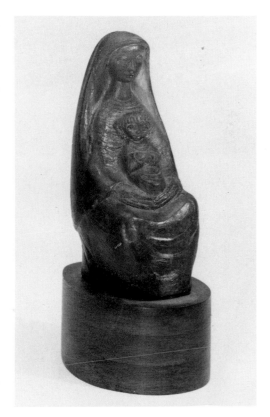

31. Edris Eckhardt, United States. 9¼″. Signed "Edris Eckhardt, 1964, Dec. 1st"

33. Edris Eckhardt, United States. 5".
    Signed "Edris Eckhardt, Edris, 1960"

◄

32. Edris Eckhardt, United States. 6¾".
    Signed "Edris Eckhardt"

◄

34. Edris Eckhardt, United States. 6".
    Signed "Edris Eckhardt"

35. Edris Eckhardt, United States. 8".
    Signed "Edris Eckhardt"

36–37.
Edris Eckhardt, United States.
(Left) 7½". Signed "Edris Eck-
hardt." *(Right)* 6½". Signed "Edris
Eckhardt"

38–39.
Edris Eckhardt, United States.
(Left) 9¾". Signed "Edris Eck-
hardt, 1964." *(Right)* 4¾". Signed
"Edris Eckhardt"

Maurice Heaton

MAURICE HEATON

Born in Neuchâtel, Switzerland, April 2, 1900

One of the truly professional American glass artists, Maurice Heaton is a third-generation glassworker. In 1914 he and his father, Clement Heaton, came to the United States and worked on stained glass church windows. In 1933 Heaton began working with enamel on glass, and over a period of many years perfected this skill. His early pieces were lighting fixtures, bowls, and dishes, for which he formed molds out of steel, using stencils for designs. By 1947 he had invented a process of fusing crushed crystals of enamel to the undersurface of the glass, and in 1961 he adapted the technique to lamination, whereby the colored enamel is fused between as many as six layers of glass.

Maurice Heaton and his wife, Berenice Van Slyke Heaton, have a daughter, Mrs. Merle G. Nelson, and a son, Hilary Van Slyke Heaton. Heaton's home, along his with kilns and workshop, is in Nyack, New York. Visitors come to his workshop there, but Heaton also periodically loads up his station wagon with a supply of his work and takes it to the various shops within driving distance, thereby serving as his own distributor.

Maurice Heaton's work has been exhibited in most of the major museums of the world, as well as being displayed in international ceramic and glass shows and in numerous one-man exhibits. It is interesting to note that an illustration of his glass appears in the *Encyclopaedia Britannica*. His work is also in the permanent collections of the Metropolitan Museum of Art, the Corning Glass Museum, the Museum of Contemporary Crafts, and numerous others. (See Color Plate 9.)

Heaton is a past vice-president of the Architectural League of New York, past president of the Rockland Foundation, and in the 1930s was a charter member and president of the Society of Designer Craftsmen, the first society of contemporary crafts in America.

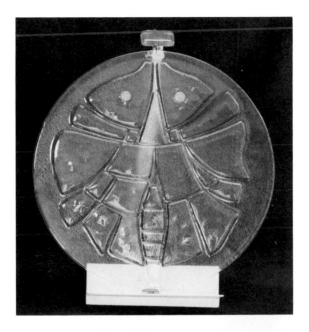

40. Maurice Heaton, United States. 10″. Signed "M.H., 1971"/"Winged Abstract"

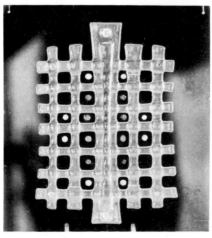

41. Maurice Heaton, United States. 11″. Signed "Maurice Heaton, 1971"/"Cross and Jewels"

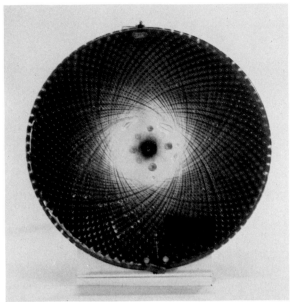

42.
Maurice Heaton, United States. 8½″. Signed "M.H., 1959"

43.
Maurice Heaton, United States. 10″. Signed "M.H., 1971"/"Sunflower Seeds"

44.
Maurice Heaton, United States. 14½″. Signed "M.H., 1954"/"Bird with Square Wings"

45.
Maurice Heaton, United States. 15″. Signed "M.H., 1959"/"Caravan"

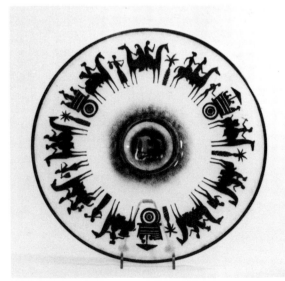

46. Maurice Heaton, United States. 10½″. Signed "M.H., 1971"/"Village"

47. Maurice Heaton, United States. 10″. Signed "M.H., 1971"/"Red Spiral on Brown and Yellow"

48. Maurice Heaton, United States. 14″. Signed "M.H."/"Whale Bones"

FRANCES and MICHAEL HIGGINS

Frances Stewart Higgins

Frances Higgins

also

and in daily use

higgins   OR

higgins

Michael Higgins

also

michael higgins

and in daily use

higgins   OR

higgins

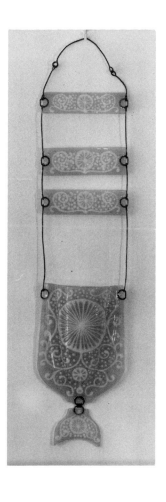

Frances and Michael Higgins, both artists in glass but each working independently in their joint shop, produce strikingly beautiful glass accentuated in the more intense colors. Rather than sculptural and blown work, they specialize in enameled design on sheet glass, frequently bent and cut into unusual shapes. Both professionals, they cater to modern tastes with colorful and well-balanced patterns. Although they work in the same shop, there is a distinct individuality in their accomplishments. Their work would fit into most contemporary homes as wall plaques, although many pieces are enhanced immeasurably with background light.

There is nothing happenstance about the Higginses' creations—each piece is seemingly well planned with a very definite subject and end result in mind. Their work is distributed through various local Chicago shops, as they live and work in the nearby Riverside, Illinois, suburb. They also exhibit for sale at numerous one- and two-day shows, open to the public. These two artists are perfectionists in design and color control, being their own severest critics. We include them as a team as they developed together in the glass field in 1948, shortly after their marriage.

Frances Stewart Higgins was born in Haddock, Jones County, Georgia, December 24, 1912. Her B.S. degree was acquired at Georgia State College for Women (now Georgia College). This was followed by summer sessions in 1936 at Columbia University Teachers College; in 1940, 1941, and 1942, at Sophie Newcomb College; 1944, Ohio State University; 1945, private tuition in weaving and jewelry; and 1946, 1947, and 1948, the Institute of Design, Chicago, following which she received a Master of Fine Arts degree. (See Color Plates 14, 16, and 17.)

Her teaching experience includes serving as critic teacher in 1934/35 at Georgia College; art teacher, 1935–44, in the junior high school in Atlanta; and assistant professor of art, 1944–48, at the University of Georgia.

49.
Frances Higgins, United States. 33″. Signed "Frances Higgins, '72"

50.
Frances Higgins, United States. 9″. Signed "Frances Higgins, 1971, Sparkler"

51.
Frances Higgins, United States. 7¾″. Signed "Frances Higgins, 1967"

Michael Higgins was born in London, England, September 29, 1908. After limited studies at Eton College and at King's College, Cambridge University, he attended night classes at London Central School of Arts and Crafts. His early work was in creative commercial advertising; then he turned to editorial and layout work on various newspapers and magazines. He soon gravitated into special political publicity work for the Labour Party of Great Britain.

Finally, renouncing all socialism and statism, he migrated to the United States in an effort to escape excessive government. Setting up a printing plant in New Orleans, he relied primarily on his own design abilities to acquire customers. When he was rejected for military service in World War II, he moved to Washington, D.C., and became Programs Officer for the Supply Mission to the Government of India. Following the war, Higgins spent some time experimenting with photographic images for reproduction, and ultimately became a teacher in, and then head of, the Visual Design Department of the Institute of Design, Chicago, before finally going into partnership with his wife as a craftsman and artist in glass. (See Color Plates 12, 13, and 15.)

52.
Michael Higgins, United States. 15¼". Signed "Michael Higgins, 1970, Red Velvet"

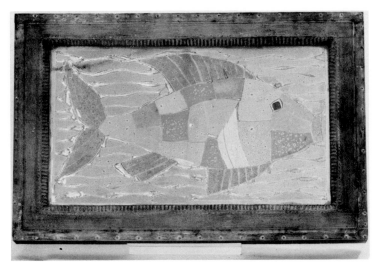

53. Michael Higgins, United States. 11". Signed "Michael Higgins, 1972"

54. Michael Higgins, United States. 14¾". Signed "Michael Higgins, 1972"

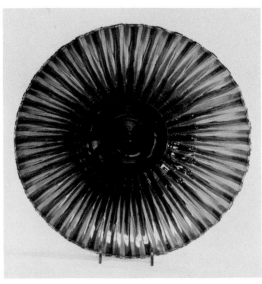

KENT IPSEN

Born in Milwaukee, Wisconsin, January 4, 1933

This well-known American glass teacher and artist and his wife, Shyla Mae, have four daughters—Laura Kay, Nina Beth, Vicki Lynn, Lisa Ann—and one son, Steven Jay. The Ipsens live in Northbrook, Illinois, a northside suburb of Chicago. Ipsen has his own workshop and kilns alongside his house, and working there with free-blown glass, he produces useful as well as beautiful creations. His pieces have no particular limit in size, shape, or surface finish. (See Color Plates 10, 11, and 18.) Undoubtedly it is because of his unusually wide capabilities that he has succeeded so well as a teacher.

Ipsen received a B.S. degree in art education at the University of Wisconsin in 1961, and worked as a public school art instructor from 1961 to 1965. After he earned an M.S. in art education in 1964, also at the University of Wisconsin, and an M.F.A. degree in ceramics and glass the following year, he became an assistant professor at Mankato State College, Mankato, Minnesota, where he introduced glass programs. In 1968, he transferred to the School of the Art Institute of Chicago, and still continues there today, an instructor in ceramics and glass. Ipsen was artist in residence during 1971/72 at The Prairie School, Racine, Wisconsin.

Since 1970 Ipsen has been president of the Illinois Craftsmen's Council and state representative to the North Central Region of the American Craft Council. He has given workshops, some seventeen to date, primarily at the college level, including the following between 1968 and 1971:

John Nelson Bergstrom Art Center and Museum, Neenah, Wisconsin, 1968
Minnesota State College, Winona, Minnesota, 1968–70
Beloit College, Beloit, Wisconsin, 1969
University of Michigan, Ann Arbor, Michigan, 1969–70
Wisconsin State College, Whitewater, Wisconsin, 1970
Arizona State University, Flagstaff, Arizona, 1971

Ipsen has also participated in twenty-six group and one-man shows. Among the better known are those at the following places:

Arts and Science Center, Nashua, New Hampshire
Chico State College, Chico, California
Chicago Art Institute, Chicago, Illinois
Ithaca College, Ithaca, New York
Long Beach Museum of Art, Long Beach, California
Louisiana State University, Baton Rouge, Louisiana
Mount Mary College, Milwaukee, Wisconsin
Sheridan College, School of Design, Port Credit, Ontario, Canada
Toledo Glass Nationals I, II, & III

55. Kent F. Ipsen, United States. 10½". Signed "Ipsen—1970"

56.
Kent F. Ipsen, United States. 14¼". Signed "Kent F. Ipsen, 1972"

57. Kent F. Ipsen, United States. 7". Signed "Kent F. Ipsen, 1972"

ROLAND JAHN

Born in Rudolstadt, Germany, 1934

Roland Jahn has a Master of Fine Arts degree from the University of Wisconsin, and has also studied art history at Friedrich-Wilhelms Universitat in Bonn, West Germany. In addition, he has studied with Leo Steppat, Abram Schlemowitz, Harvey Littleton, and Don Reitz.

After conducting workshops at the Penland School of Crafts Penland, North Carolina, in 1969 and 1970, he became assistant professor at the Philadelphia School of Art, in the Craft Department. Besides teaching glass and ceramics, he works in cast bronze, primarily in the sculptural and functional approaches. (See Color Plate 20.) He is represented in many private collections as well as in:

Art Museum, Wilmington, Delaware

Brooks Memorial Gallery, Memphis, Tennessee

Corning Museum of Glass, Corning, New York

Frank Lloyd Wright Headquarters of the Johnson Foundation, Racine, Wisconsin

Museum of Art, Newark, New Jersey
Philadelphia Museum of Art, Philadelphia, Pennsylvania
University of Wisconsin, Statistics Department Collection

SHOWS AND EXHIBITIONS:
Ball State University, Muncie, Indiana
Everson Museum of Art, Syracuse
Milwaukee Art Center, Milwaukee, Wisconsin
Philadelphia Civic Center
Sheridan College, Oakville, Ontario, Canada
Smithsonian Institution Traveling Exhibition
Toledo Glass National II
Wichita Museum, Wichita, Kansas
Wisconsin Salon, 1965

58. Roland Jahn, United States. 10″. Signed "R. Jahn, 1971"

RUTH MARIA KILBY

Born in Czechoslovakia

Married to Robert A. Kilby and currently working and residing in New York City, Ruth Kilby has a well-founded background in art. Following graduation from the Real Gymnasium, Karlsbad, Czechoslovakia, she spent two years in Paris at the Femme de Demain, receiving a degree in design and art. After continuing her studies in Berlin, she worked as a designer in Europe and the United States until 1948, when she began devoting her full time to experiments in glass.

Primarily, her work revolves around the varying effects of light passing through glass, not only in single-layer stained glass windows but also in fusing multiple layers of glass, thereby avoiding the necessity of leading. She has been successful in producing paintings in fused glass that can hang in the home. When lit with background light, the three-dimensional quality of these pieces is projected to the viewer. Her fusion work quite frequently consists of large chunks, as well as smaller pebbles and dust, polished as well as coarse. Ruth Kilby uses these various parts as though they were an application of paint, and many new and pleasing lines and color combinations result. (See Color Plate 19.)

In 1958, Mrs. Kilby made two murals for the main lounge of the S.S. *Atlantic*, and in 1964 twenty panels carrying out the theme "Joie de Vivre" for the entrance doors of the French Pavilion at the New York World's Fair. Her work has appeared in a traveling show of the American Federation of Art and at the Corning Museum of Glass, as well as in the following exhibitions:

One-man show, Ward Eggleston, New York, 1953

One-man show, Lowe Museum of Art, University of Miami, 1954

One-man show, Architectural League, New York, 1955

Art Institute of Chicago, Society of Contemporary Art, 1957, 1960

59.
Ruth Kilby, United States. 18″. Signed "Ruth Kilby, 1962, Jungle"

60.
Ruth Kilby, United States. 16″. Signed "Ruth Kilby, 1969, Search in the round"

Frank L. Kulasiewicz (signature)

FRANK KULASIEWICZ

An extensive background of study, travel and training has certainly been important to the success of this artist in the fields of ceramics and glass. Kulasiewicz received B.F.A. and B.S. degrees at Wisconsin State College in 1953 and an M.A. degree at the University of Wisconsin in 1956 (after being in the army for eighteen months, stationed near Nancy, France). He then spent some fifteen months in Japan, Thailand, Singapore, Hong Kong, and Cambodia during 1957/8, teaching and supervising arts and crafts. Proceeding to France, Holland, Denmar, Norway, Sweden, and Italy, he continued in the academic-teaching field for another twenty-two months. His own studies included considerable work in Germany: at the Offenbach Werkkunstschule in 1961; the Walter Merkelbach Fabrik-Hohr-Greenzhausen, 1960–61; and the Leica school in Wetzlar, in photography, 1960. In addition to receiving the Japan Society Travel Grant in 1966, he was the recipient of a Tiffany grant in glass sculpture in 1967. His travels took him to the Mexican crafts centers in the summers of 1968 and 1969.

Kulasiewicz has also taught at the Milwaukee Downer College in Wisconsin; the University of Wisconsin; New Mexico State University; Columbia University; Saugatuck Summer Art School, Michigan; Montclair State College, New Jersey; Northwestern University; University of Texas, Austin, Texas; and in the New York City public schools.

In 1964, while teaching at Northwestern University, Frank Kulasiewicz set up his first glass studio and worked at developing small, easily portable glass furnaces. The studio-factory was moved in 1966 to New Mexico, where for five years he worked on designing and producing glass equipment and tools, as well as creating original glass formulas. His present studio is in Austin, Texas, where with his wife, Carol, a fine weaver and glassworker herself, he works in blown glass and metal sculpture combinations. (See Color Plates 21 and 22.)

61. Frank Kulasiewicz, United States. 6½″. Signed "External Sphincter, 1969, Kulasiewicz"

Among some forty exhibitions and shows in which Kulasiewicz's work has appeared, the following stand out:

America House, New York
Baltimore Art Museum, Baltimore, Maryland
Carnegie Institute Invitational, Pittsburgh, Pennsylvania
Contemporary Crafts Museum, New York
First National Invitational Glass Show, San Jose, California
Gallery of Fine Arts, Dallas, Texas
Library of Congress International Travel Show
Momentum Show, Chicago
National Academy, New York
New York World's Fair
Ontario Crafts Foundation Contemporary Glass Invitational, Canada
Smithsonian Institution Traveling Exhibition
Toledo Museum of Art National Shows
"Young Americans," Traveling Show

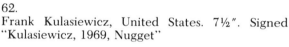

62.
Frank Kulasiewicz, United States. 7½". Signed "Kulasiewicz, 1969, Nugget"

65. ▶
Frank Kulasiewicz, United States. 9¼". Signed "Kulasiewicz, 1970, Tripod"

63.
Frank Kulasiewicz, United States. 6½". Signed "Kulasiewicz, Ortolan pullet lanced by a directed external sphincter"

64.
Frank Kulasiewicz, United States. 4". Signed "Kulasiewicz, Embryonic Ruby, 1965"

DOMINICK LABINO

Born in Clarion County, Pennsylvania, December 4, 1910

One of the most frequent questions asked us by collectors of art glass today is: "Who, in your opinion, will be the collectible artists of tomorrow?" It would be difficult to name any one individual on the scene today who qualifies for this distinction to the degree that "Nick" Labino does. In making such a choice, one has to consider originality, ability, knowledge, the quality and quantity of the artist's production, and his public exposure, distribution, and acceptance. Labino certainly qualifies in all these respects.

Financially independent, Labino has four furnaces constantly in operation in a fireproof building on a farm near Grand Rapids, Ohio, just south of Toledo. Since he hires no apprentices, and has no help other than his wife Libby (Elizabeth Smith Labino), there is no one to answer to, only his own standards for the perfection and quality of his glass. Labino's productions are not stereotyped—each piece is unique, and personally finished. In his striving for perfection, he refuses to use old or leftover batches of glass, but discards them in order to avoid internally created stresses.

All records are meticulously kept by Libby Labino—not only those pertinent to the overall operation of the works, but also relating to the actual chemical and physical details of the various types of pieces. The quantity produced may be from eight pieces on up, on any given day; their quality is never a matter of "luck"— originality of internal and external design is the result of careful planning and skilled execution.

Since commencing in 1929 with industrial experience in glass, Labino has never been out of the field as a participant. On the contrary, he has been one of its leaders, even going so far as to design practical working kilns used by studio glassworkers today. Until his retirement in 1965, he was vice-president and director of research for Johns-Manville fiber glass; he is still affiliated with the company as a research consultant.

As indicated, a considerable quantity of Labino's work has been offered on the market, to be only too quickly gobbled up by collectors. This in itself would, without question, indicate public acceptance. But although all Labino's creations are potentially highly desirable collectibles, that in no way precludes many other contemporary artists from being sought after, as the work they are now producing and will produce in the future becomes rare and constantly more eagerly bought by the collecting community all over the world. Many artists on the scene today are well bought up; many are limited by the small amount of work they produce. As a matter of fact, no one included in this book lacks the potential, in our estimation, of becoming a collectible great.

Labino was educated at Allegheny Vocational High School, and Carnegie Institute of Technology in Pittsburgh, as well as at the Toledo Museum of Art, School of Design. He holds fifty-seven United States patents and several hundred in foreign countries. Three of his developments for glass fibers pertaining to insulation were used in the Apollo spacecraft. Labino's *Visual Art in Glass* was published in 1968; he is also the author of an article on Egyptian Eighteeth Dynasty hollow-vessel glass made on a sand core (1500 B.C.), which appeared in the *Journal of Glass Studies*, vol. VIII, 1966, published by the Corning Museum of Glass.

In 1963, on his farm, Labino began to work with glass as an art form, doing freehand blowing. He not only designs and builds his own furnaces but also annealing ovens, glassblowing tools, and finishing equipment. His laboratory is well equipped for testing the properties of glass, and his serious research into the development of color has resulted in glass compositions with unusual and exciting effects. Thus, with a profound command of the chemistry of glass, he is able to achieve colors that are uniquely his own, and visual effects that are dependent on, and enhanced by, the high quality of the glass itself. (See Color Plates 23 through 29.)

For the first Glass Workshop held by the Toledo Museum of Art in 1962, Labino designed the furnace and furnished the glass for the first experiments in studio glassblowing. More to the point, he has made available technical knowledge on the formulating of glass, as well as on the design and construction of furnaces practical for studio craftsmen. Four seminars on glassblowing in his own studio-workshop have been held for the Toledo Museum of Art, and he has helped in setting up glassblowing classes at colleges and universities.

In 1968, Labino was named Honorary Curator of Glass by the Toledo Museum of Art, and in 1969 he was honored with a citation from the Martha Kinney Cooper Ohioana Library Association for distinguished service to Ohio in the field of creative art as an internationally recognized glass artist and inventor. His monumental polychrome glass mural "Vitrana" stands at the entrance to the New Glass Gallery at the Toledo Museum of Art. It was the authors' privilege to know of, and to observe the time-consuming assemblage of, this magnificent accomplishment, shown for the first time in 1970.

Nick and Libby Labino have two children, Jane Labino Black and Mary K. Labino Garn, as well as four grandchildren—Kathryn Ann, Edward Dominick, Julie Elizabeth, and John Michael.

Thirty-eight museums, most of international repute, have examples of Labino glass in their permanent collections. A few of them are listed here:

Arizona State University, Tempe, Arizona
Bennington Museum, Bennington, Vermont
Chrysler Museum of Art, Norfolk, Virginia
Cincinnati Museum of Art
Cleveland Museum of Art
Corning Museum of Glass, Corning, New York
Detroit Institute of Art
Fowler Museum, Los Angeles, California
Milan Historical Museum, Milan, Ohio
National Glass Museum, Leerdam, The Netherlands
"Objects U.S.A.," The Johnson Wax Collection, Racine, Wisconsin
Pilkington Museum of Glass, St. Helens, Lancashire, England
Smithsonian Institution, Washington, D.C.
Toledo Museum of Art

Since 1963 Labino has participated in more than 120 exhibitions, so only a few of them likewise can be listed here:

Alfred University, Alfred, New York, Invitational One-man Show
Association of Arts and Crafts Invitational Glass Exhibit, Boston
John Nelson Bergstrom Art Center and Museum, Neenah, Wisconsin
Biennial Ceramics and Decorative Arts Exhibition, Wichita, Kansas
Bowling Green State University, one-man show, Bowling Green, Ohio
Corning Museum of Glass, "Dominick Labino—A Retrospective Exhibition, 1964–1969"
Forsythe Gallery, Ann Arbor, Michigan, Invitational One-man Show
Institute of Contemporary Art, Boston
John Michael Kohler Arts Center, Sheboygan, Wisconsin
Museum of Contemporary Crafts, New York, Exhibition Permanent Collection
Museum of Fine Arts, Houston, Texas
Nelson Gallery, Atkins Museum Invitational Exhibition, Kansas City
Oshkosh Public Museum, Oshkosh, Wisconsin
San Jose College Invitational Glass Exhibition, San Jose, California
Scripps College Invitational Ceramics Exhibition, Claremont, California

In the brief period of only ten years, Labino has received over thirty awards and prizes for selective and outstanding work, as well as many "purchase-awards" as pieces were acquired for permanent collections.

66. John Conard Lewis, United States. 4¾".
Signed "Lewis, 1971, Moon Bottle"

JOHN CONARD LEWIS

Born in Berkeley, California, 1942

Not content with glass in its traditionally functional form, John Conard Lewis, working from furnaces of his own design, attempts to take advantage of the unique possibilities of glass as a purely sculptural medium. Using an unlimited palette of colors to obtain complex compositions, he imbues his glass with fanciful qualities, as is quite evident in his Moon Bottles. His simple ovoid forms bring out a variety of surface effects that suggest landscape motifs, an endless variety of seascapes, and the depths of the sky. This work by Lewis is not only an exciting presentation of design, albeit well controlled, but strikes the observer as an important contribution to giving scenic depth to glass. Undoubtedly Lewis's Moon Bottles will achieve an enviable place in future glass collections. (See Color Plate 31.)

Educated at the University of California, from which he received an M.A. degree in 1970, Lewis, who is represented by Sterling Associates, Palo Alto, has received the following awards:

Corning Glass Museum, sole purchase prize, 1970

Designer Craftsmen's Award, Richmond Art Center, California, 1969

First National Invitational Handblown Glass Exhibition, Tacoma Art Museum, 1971

Sixth Annual All-State College Competition, California, 1970

EXHIBITIONS:

College of San Mateo, San Mateo, California, 1970

Long Beach Museum of Art, Long Beach, California, 1971

Pasadena Museum of Art, Pasadena, California, 1970

Richmond Art Center, Richmond, California, 1970

Tacoma Art Museum, Tacoma, Washington, 1971

MARVIN LIPOFSKY

Born in Barrington, Illinois, 1938

Identified as one of the first American glass artists of today to depart from traditional forms in glass art, Marvin Lipofsky has been internationally recognized and accepted for his personally creative achievements. These have encompassed complicated sculpture as well as unusual surface applications to his exciting glass forms.

Originally a member of Harvey Littleton's first glass-workshop at the University of Wisconsin in 1962, Lipofsky subsequently acquired M.S. and M.F.A. degrees in sculpture (in 1964). Prior to that, he had received a B.F.A. degree in industrial design at the University of Illinois. From 1964 to the present, he has been an assistant professor in the Department of Design at the University of California. During that same period he has also been a visiting lecturer or instructor at:

University of Wisconsin, Madison, Wisconsin, 1964

Haystack Mountain School, Deer Isle, Maine, 1967

California College of Arts and Crafts, Oakland, 1967

San Francisco Art Institute, 1968

Gerriet Rietveld Academie, Amsterdam, The Netherlands, 1970

Bazalel Academy of Art and Design, Jerusalem, Israel, 1971

Lipofsky is represented in over twenty-three important collections, some of which follow here:

Frauenau Glass Museum, Frauenau, West Germany

The Johnson Wax Collection, "Objects U.S.A.," Racine, Wisconsin

Milwaukee Art Center, Milwaukee, Wisconsin

Musée d'Art Contemporain, Skopje, Yugoslavia

Museum Boymans–Van Beuningen, Rotterdam, The Netherlands

Museum of Contemporary Crafts, New York

National Museum of Glass, Leerdam, The Netherlands

Stedelijke Museum, Amsterdam, The Netherlands

Toledo Museum of Art

In addition to twelve one-man shows, Lipofsky has received awards for his work from fifteen well-known institutions, quite a remarkable amount of personal recognition in a most sought after field, as well as having his work displayed in thirty competitive exhibitions. Among some eighty invitational exhibitions over the years, practically all of which were noteworthy, he has participated in the following:

Group Sculpture Exhibition, Devorah Sherman Gallery, Chicago, 1964

Media Exhibit (glass), 1st World Congress of Craftsmen, Columbia University, New York, 1964

67.
Marvin Lipofsky, United States. 3¾".
Signed "Lipofsky, 1966–67"

California Crafts IV Invitational, E. B. Crocker Gallery, Sacramento, 1965

Creative Casting (glass sculpture), Museum West, San Francisco 1965

Society of Art and Crafts, Boston, 1966

California State Art Commission, traveling exhibition, 1966

Hayward Festival of the Arts, Hayward, California, 1967

College of Marin, Sculpture Invitational, Kentfield, California, 1968

Flint Institute of Arts, Flint, Michigan, 1969

National Museum of Glass, Leerdam, The Netherlands, 1969

"Objects: U.S.A.," The Johnson Collection, Racine, Wisconsin, 1969

Town Museum, Arnhem, The Netherlands, 1970

"Attitudes," The Brooklyn Museum, Brooklyn, New York, 1970

Pasadena Museum of Art, Pasadena, California, 1971

Tacoma Art Museum, Tacoma, Washington, 1971

National Museum of Glass, Leerdam, The Netherlands, 1972

Not only is Lipofsky talented in both glass work and teaching; he is also a successful lecturer with a record seventy appearances in Europe and the United States. In addition to personal appearances, this gifted individual has been active in radio and television, and is one of the most sought after guest artists and leaders at the various international forums.

HARVEY LITTLETON

Born in Corning, New York
Married September 6, 1947 to Bess Tamura
Children: Carol, Thomas, John, and Maurine

Among the first artists in the United States to start working in glass as a craft medium, Harvey Littleton has been one of the leaders and masters in the field. The utmost recognition must be given to Littleton when one stops to realize how many of the currently top artists indicate they have studied studio-glassmaking with him. And the Littleton name is as well known in Europe as it is in his own country. Not only in the academic field but also in his dynamic and and novel approach to glass sculpture, he is among the leaders.

Littleton effectively utilizes all the inherent qualities of glass so that his work is a truly personal expression of genuine artistry. His original forms and complex shapes began to appear in 1964, and as the years have gone by, his combining of black and white, as well as beautiful and subtle color combinations, has aroused great interest on the part of collectors and museums alike. (See Color Plates 32 and 33.)

From 1951 to the present, Littleton has been associated with the University of Wisconsin as a teacher in art education and studio glassmaking. He has been invited to many workshops and been the recipient of six research grants. After attending the Brighton School of Art in England in 1945, he went on to acquire a B.D. degree at the University of Michigan in 1947 and an M.F.A. degree at the

68. Harvey K. Littleton, United States. 6½″. Signed "H. K. Littleton, 1964, Non Bottle"

◄

69. Harvey K. Littleton, United States. 8¾″. Signed "H. K. Littleton, 1969, Brown Eye"

Cranbrook Academy of Art in 1951. His work is represented in over thirty museums, including these:

Corning Museum of Glass, Corning, New York

Detroit Art Institute, Detroit, Michigan

Groningen Museum, Groningen, The Netherlands

Kunstgewerbe Museum, Cologne, West Germany

Museum of Modern Art, New York

Smithsonian Institution, Washington, D.C.

Toledo Museum of Art, Toledo, Ohio

Victoria and Albert Museum, London, England

Fifteen national and international awards have come the way of Harvey Littleton. He has had forty one-man shows, including an important showing at the Corning Museum of Glass, as well as participating in numerous traveling group shows. In invitational and competitive exhibitions, this important glassman has shown more than ninety times. The following list indicates his importance:

John Nelson Bergstrom Art Center and Museum, Neenah, Wisconsin, 1967

Boston Society of Arts and Crafts, 1966

Brooks Memorial Art Center, Memphis, Tennessee, 1963

Dallas Museum of Fine Arts, 1967

Exhibition (13th Triennial) of Architecture and Decorative Art, Palazzo dell-'Arte, Milan, Italy, 1964

First International Exposition of Ceramics, Cannes, France, 1956

Groningen Museum, Groningen, The Netherlands, 1970

International Cultural Exchange Exhibition, Palais de Ariana, Geneva, Switzerland, 1960

Kohler Art Center, Sheboygan, Wisconsin, 1968

Munich International Crafts Fair, 1968

Museum of Contemporary Crafts, New York, 1967

Museum of Modern Art, New York, 1967

Museum West of the American Craftsmen's Council, 1965

National Glass Museum, Leerdam, The Netherlands

"Objects U.S.A.," The Johnson Wax Collection, Racine, Wisconsin, 1969

Scripps College 24th Ceramic Invitational Exhibition, Claremont, California

Sheridan College, School of Design, Port Credit, Canada, 1970

Toledo Glass National III, 1970

U.S.I.A. Traveling Exhibition of American Crafts, Latin America, 1965

University of Alberta, Canada, 1965: "Littleton and Eisch Contemporary Glass"

World Agricultural Fair, New Delhi, India, U.S. Pavilion, 1959

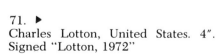

CHARLES GERALD LOTTON

Born in Elizabethtown, Illinois, October 21, 1935
Wife: Mary
Children: David, Daniel, John, and Rachel

Working at his own furnace and annealing oven, in his own workshop, Lotton has been involved in glass for only a few years, but in that short period of time has shown remarkable results. Much of his work is reminiscent of the Art Nouveau period—including not only beautifully decorated, iridescent finishes combined with flowing designs, but also some very accomplished internally decorated pieces of great promise. At the present time his sole representatives are Paul and Chloe Nassau, 220 East 57th Street, New York City. (See Color Plate 40.)

70.
Charles Lotton, United States. 5″.
Signed "Lotton—1972"

71. ▶
Charles Lotton, United States. 4″.
Signed "Lotton, 1972"

JIM LUNDBERG

Born in Chicago, Illinois, 1948

Ten years' work as a traditional potter, along with Lundberg's obsession with the Art Nouveau period, has influenced the underlying style of this fine glassmaker. Introduced to glassblowing by Dr. R. C. Fritz in 1968, he shortly turned professional and in 1970 opened his own private glass studio. His efforts have been in the direction of technical mastery and dexterous manipulation of fluid glass. Many of his experiments in the use of reactive metal oxides have brought unusually pleasing results. (See Color Plate 37.)

Lundberg's interest in ceramics developed while he was still in junior high school; it has never abated. In 1967 he entered San Jose State College as a ceramics major, graduating with a B.A. degree in 1971. Next came graduate study and research in England, Holland, France, Spain, Italy, and Germany, followed by additional time spent at the Corning Glass Library, Alfred University, and the Toledo Museum of Art. In 1972 he acquired his master's degree in Art at San Jose State College. In this short period he has had notable exhibits:

"California Design XI"
Coast Gallery, Monterey, California
Fairtree Gallery of Contemporary Crafts, New York
"Media '71" and "Media '72," Walnut Creek, California
Oakland Museum of Art, Oakland, California
S.F.P.A. De Young Museum Biennial, San Francisco
"The Egg and The I," Los Angeles
"The Renaissance Pleasure Faire"

72. Jim Lundberg, United States. 8¾″. Signed "Lundberg—5/20/1972"

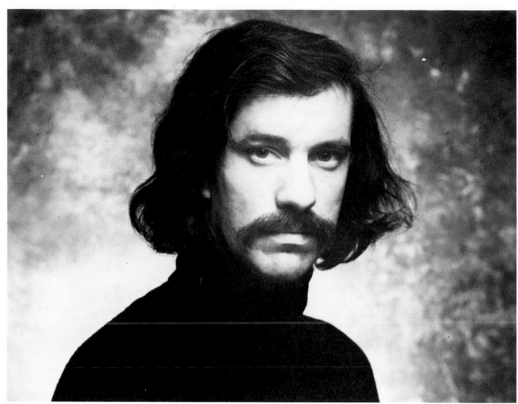

STEVEN MILDWOFF

Born in New York City, 1940

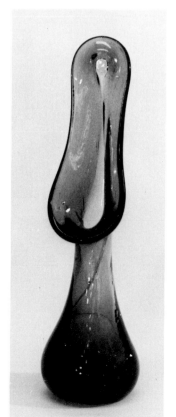

Studies at the Art Student League in New York and at the Museum of Modern Art, in courses dealing with the fusing and laminating of glass, started Mildwoff in the field of glassmaking. While living in Europe shortly afterward, he studied at the Academy of Art in Florence, Italy. Next followed a job in Mexico City with a factory that manufactured blown glass globes for lighting. Mildwoff built a production bending lehr and all the related facilities, including glass-cutting machines, drilling machines, and the silk screens used in decoration, in addition to training new personnel.

In 1965 he was invited by Harvey Littleton to come to the University of Wisconsin for a year to teach decorating techniques of blown glass, after which—in 1966—he built his own studio in New York. The following year Mildwoff attended the Toledo Museum of Art glass seminar, under the direction of Dominick Labino, and then spent the year 1968 working in various Midwestern glass factories. In Fort Smith, Arkansas, he was the gaffer in a hand-shop. New York, however, became his

73. Steven Mildwoff, United States. 10½". Signed "Steven Mildwoff, 1969"

45

gravitational point once again, and he continues to operate there and blow glass in his own studio. (See Color Plate 39.)

EXHIBITIONS:

Corning Museum of Glass, Corning, New York, 1959

Museum of Contemporary Crafts, Design for Production Show, New York, 1964

Museum of Modern Art, New York

Toledo Glass Nationals I and II, 1966 and 1968

University of Nebraska, Lincoln, Nebraska

74.
Steven Mildwoff, United States. 6¼". Signed "Steven Mildwoff, S.M., B–1235–67." 1967

75–76–77.
Steven Mildwoff, United States. *(Left)* 4". Signed "Steven Mildwoff, 1968." *(Center)* 2½". Signed "Steven Mildwoff." *(Right)* 3". Signed "Steven Mildwoff, 1968"

Bowling Green State University, Bowling Green, Ohio, 1966

Chicago Art Institute School

George Walter Vincent Smith Art Museum, Springfield, Massachusetts, 1971–72

Museum of Contemporary Crafts, New York, 1967

Philadelphia Art Alliance, 1970

Myers is represented in a number of private collections. In addition to his many other activities, he has also conducted glass seminars as well as around fifteen workshops. It would be difficult, in fact, to overestimate Joel Myers's influence on and importance in the contemporary glass field. (See Color Plates 38, 41, and 42.)

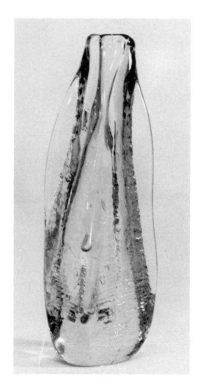

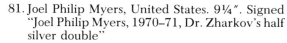

80. Joel Philip Myers, United States. 15½″. Signed "Blown by Joel Philip Myers at Blenko, 1965"

81. Joel Philip Myers, United States. 9¼″. Signed "Joel Philip Myers, 1970–71, Dr. Zharkov's half silver double"

ROBERT E. NAESS

Born in Morristown, New Jersey, December 27, 1943

In 1962 Robert Naess entered the University of California, Berkeley. He was graduated in 1969 with a B.A. degree in sculpture, and in 1970 earned his M.A. degree. In
the meantime, in addition to his normal academic life on campus, he continued his
early interest in machinery, design, and the function of engines. With only a brief
commitment to architecture, Naess began doing metal sculptural work in his workshop, and shortly after being introduced to glassmaking, he spent more and more
time using glass as a medium for his sculptural ideas. His glass constructions in the
shapes of articles of daily use, but with whimsical implications, have attracted considerable attention to his work. (See Color Plates 43 and 44.)

   Following graduation in California, Naess spent the summer of 1970 working
in the Venini glass company in Murano, Italy, returning to the United States to give
numerous workshops at Penland, North Carolina; San Mateo College; California

College of Arts and Crafts; and the University of California, Berkeley. For the past several years he has been teaching basic art courses at the Kansas City Art Institute. His exhibitions include:

A.S.U.C. Gallery, University of California, Berkeley, 1969

Boston Museum of Fine Arts, Wellington-Ivest Collection, 1968

California Crafts VI, Sacramento, California, 1969; award

Chico State College, Invitational IV, California, 1969

College of Arts and Crafts, Oakland, California, 1970

First Invitational Sculpture Exhibition, Berkeley, 1969; award

Joslyn Art Museum, Omaha, Nebraska, 1972

Kemper Gallery, Glass, Clay, Fiber Invitational, Kansas City, 1972

Monte Vista Invitational, California, 1969

Museum of Contemporary Crafts, Hawaii and California, 1969

Scripps College Invitational, Pomona, California, 1968; award

Toledo Glass National II, 1968

82.
Robert E. Naess, United States. 5″. Signed "American brain cornucopia, Robert E. Naess, Berkeley, 1970"

83.
Robert E. Naess, United States. 3″. Signed "R. Naess, '69, Berkeley, Calif., Unicorn Hoof Cup"

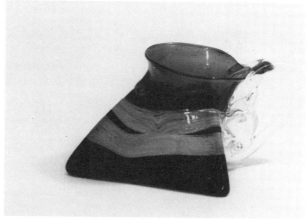

KIMRIE T. NEWCOMB

Born in Detroit, Michigan, November 27, 1945

84. Kim Newcomb, United States. 5″. Signed "Newcomb, 1972"

Recognized for his blown-glass objects as well as his ability to express himself in sculptural shapes, Kim Newcomb shows great promise in the creation of fine and unique pieces. His education started at Foothill College in 1966; subsequently he received his B.A. and M.A. degrees from San Jose State College in 1968 and 1969 respectively. The year 1970 found him attending the University of California at Berkeley and California College of Arts and Crafts.

After a year as instructor in art at Foothill College, he spent the following two years performing the same function at the University of Illinois. In addition to being a guest lecturer on numerous occasions, he has been quite active in giving glass demonstrations.

Newcomb has received awards from Shasta College, Redding, California, 1969; Crocker Art Gallery, Sacramento, 1969; San Mateo College, San Mateo, California, 1968; and San Jose City College, in 1968. He is represented in a number of public collections, such as that of the Johnson Wax Company; the American Craftsmen's Council, New York City; Shasta College, Redding, California; San Jose City College; and the Huntington Galleries, West Virginia. (See Color Plate 45.)

85–86–87–88.
Kim Newcomb, United States. *(Left)* 7¾". Signed "Newcomb, 1971." *(Center Left)* 6¾". Signed "Newcomb, 1971." *(Center Right)* 8¾". Signed "Newcomb, 1971." *(Right)* 8½". Signed "Newcomb, 1971"

The following are some of the many exhibitions in which Newcomb has participated:

Bloomfield Art Association, Birmingham, Michigan
Crocker Art Gallery, Sacramento, California
National Invitational, Hawaii
Northern Illinois University, De Kalb, Illinois
"Objects U.S.A.," the Johnson Wax Corporation, Racine, Wisconsin, 1969–71
Pasadena Museum, Pasadena, California
San Mateo College, San Mateo, California
Shasta College, Redding, California
Sheboygan Arts Foundation, Sheboygan, Wisconsin
Walnut Creek Art Center, Walnut Creek, California

MARK PEISER

1971

Born in Chicago, Illinois, January 8, 1939
Wife: Jane Roslin Peiser, ceramist, 1962
Daughter: Martha Jane, 1971

89. Mark Peiser, United States. 4". Signed "Mark Peiser, 1970"

Mark C. Peiser

MARK COMFORT PEISER

MARK PEISER 1971

MARK PEISER 1972

MARK PEISER 1973

MARK PEISER 1969

Not satisfied with less than the perfection achieved by personal experimentation, Mark Peiser contributes to the field of glass not only fine miniatures and larger sculptural pieces, but a sense of balanced decoration in his colorful work. This has resulted in his being widely accepted by collectors, who acquire his work through numerous art galleries in the United States. His wife, an outstanding ceramist, is as well recognized. Peiser's shop is well laid out and fitted with new and self-built equipment.

Having majored in electrical engineering at Purdue University (1955–57) and then acquired his B.S. degree at the Institute of Design of the Illinois Institute of Technology (1958–61), Peiser spent another two years, from 1965 to 1967, at the De Paul University School of Music. Following the period at Purdue, he entered the business world as a machine designer, product designer, and finally director of three-dimensional display; then he ran his own product design office to finance himself through music school. In the course of this work he became exposed to glassblowing, which seemed to give him the ideal opportunity of planning, creating, and realizing his own personal inspirations without having to answer to anyone else.

After only a five-week course in glassblowing at the Penland School of Crafts in 1967, Peiser became a resident craftsman at Penland. During the following two years he completed his own workshop. With his fine scientific background, rather than follow the methods of others Mark Peiser constantly runs his own tests and experiments, and although sometimes his findings are already common knowledge, this personal experimentation has broadened his abilities. Discovering for himself the limits of the various materials has increased his awareness of their possibilities —and resulted in his turning out some extremely fine work. His business background has also aided Peiser in becoming one of the more successful producers of art glass.

Because of the quality of his work, Peiser is represented in a number of outstanding collections, including those at the Smithsonian Institution, the Art Institute of Chicago, the Johnson Wax Company, and the Peggy Guggenheim Museum in Venice. (See Color Plates 46 and 47.) He has exhibited at a great many shows (the following is a partial list), and has an unusually high record of prize awards:

America House, Birmingham, Michigan, 1970

"Appalachian Corridors," Charleston, West Virginia, 1968, 1970

90.
Mark Peiser, United States. 5½". Signed "Mark Peiser, 1971"

91. ▶
Mark Peiser, United States. 6". Signed "Mark Peiser, 1971"

Burpee Art Center, Rockford, Illinois, 1970
Gainesville, Florida, Fine Arts Show, 1969
Kansas City Art Institute, Kansas City, Kansas, 1972
Kohler Art Center, Sheboygan, Wisconsin, 1972
Lakefront Art Festival, Milwaukee, Wisconsin, 1971
N.E.E.C.A. Glass Invitational, University of Wisconsin, 1970
St. Augustine, Florida, Fine Arts Show, 1968, 1969, 1971
Sheldon Swope Art Gallery, Terre Haute, Indiana
Sheridan College, School of Design, Port Credit, Ontario, 1970
Southwest Craft Center, San Antonio, Texas, 1971
University of Georgia, Athens, Georgia, 1969
University of Minnesota, St. Cloud, Minnesota, 1971
Winter Park (Florida) Arts and Crafts Show, 1968, 1969, 1970

JACK A. SCHMIDT

Born in *Toledo, Ohio, December, 1945*

Following graduation from Bowling Green State University, Bowling Green, Ohio, Jack Schmidt spent four years in teaching and intensive glass studies at the Toledo Museum of Art, Penland School of Crafts, Alfred University, and Illinois State University, Normal, Illinois, where he is currently working with that fine artist Joel Philip Myers. He has also taught glassmaking at Haystack Hinckley, Hinckley, Maine, and at the Naples School of Arts and Crafts, Inc., Naples, New York. (See Color Plate 48.)

In addition to assisting in many glass workshops and receiving two awards in 1972 from Beaux Arts Designer, Craftsman, as the "Illinois State Outstanding Craftsman," Schmidt has exhibited in the following shows:

Alma Perlis Gallery, Allentown, Pennsylvania
Butler Institute of American Art, Youngstown, Ohio, 1969
Hanamura-Hagopian Invitational, 1970, Detroit, Michigan
Mid-states Craft Exhibit, Evansville, Indiana, 1972
New York State Craftsmen Show, Ithaca, New York, 1970, 1971
Scarabaeus Limited, New York
Smithsonian Institution sponsored traveling show
Southern Tier Arts and Crafts Show, Corning, New York, 1970
Toledo Glass National, 1968

93.
Jack A. Schmidt, United States. 9¾″. Signed "Schmidt, '70"

92.
Jack A. Schmidt, United States. 11″. Signed "Jack Schmidt"

JAMES L. TANNER

Born in Jacksonville, Florida, July 22, 1941
Wife: Sandra M. Tanner, M.F.A.

With the encouragement of his high school art teacher, James Tanner studied fine arts at Florida A & M University and received a B.A. degree there in 1964. He spent the following summer at Aspen School of Contemporary Art, Aspen, Colorado, on a scholarship, before enrolling at the University of Wisconsin, where he earned the degrees of M.S. and M.F.A. in 1966 and 1967. At Wisconsin he studied under the guidance of Hal Lotterman in painting, Don Reitz in ceramics, and Harvey Littleton in glass. In 1968, after becoming associate professor of ceramics and glassworking at

Mankato State College in Mankato, Minnesota, Tanner set up the first glass laboratory there. At present, he continues to teach at Mankato. (See Color Plate 50.)

Tanner was featured in a ninety-minute ABC-TV news special sponsored by the Johnson Wax Company in 1970. He has done summer teaching at Walsh College in Canton, Ohio (1968, 1969, 1970), as well as at Penland School of Crafts (1970). A fluent speaker, he is sought as a lecturer and discussion panelist. Among his exhibitions are the following:

Carnegie-Mellon University, "Glass Sculpture Invitational," Pittsburgh, 1969
Cedar Rapids Art Center, Cedar Rapids, Iowa, 1970
Fall River Art Center, Fall River, Massachusetts, 1969, 1970
John Michael Kohler Art Center, Sheboygan, Wisconsin, 1971
Lee Nordness Galleries, "Twelve Afro-American Artists," New York, 1969
Long Beach Museum of Art, Long Beach, California, 1971–72
Museum of Contemporary Crafts, "Young Americans," New York, 1968
"Objects U.S.A.," the Johnson Wax Collection, Racine, Wisconsin
Rochester Art Center, Rochester, Minnesota, 1972
Toledo Glass National II, 1968

94.
James L. Tanner, United States. 8½". Signed "Tanner, 1971, King's Hat"

95.
James L. Tanner, United States. 4½". Signed "1972, Tanner"

GEORGE J. THIEWES

Born in Waseca, Minnesota, May 26, 1943

Graduation from Mankato State College with a B.S. degree in 1969 after seven years of studies at the Minneapolis School of Art, University of Minnesota, and St. Cloud State College, St. Cloud, Minnesota, was the prelude to Thiewes's becoming a graduate assistant at the University of Northern Illinois. In the fall of 1970 he attended the Art Institute of Chicago, and received a teaching assistantship while working on his M.F.A. During this period he taught at William Rainey Harger College, Palatine, Illinois, and was guest artist at numerous workshops.

In spite of the comparative brevity of his career, Thiewes has been quite prolific. The following list represents a sampling of the exhibitions to which he has been invited:

"Arts U.S.A. II," Northern Illinois University, De Kalb, 1971

Bennington (Vermont) Art Fair, 1971

Craft Commitment Institute, Minnesota, 1970, 1971, 1972
"Crafts 1971," Cleveland, Ohio
Fox River (Illinois) Art Festival, 1970, 1971
"Glass I," Bloomfield, Michigan, 1971
Lake Front Fair, Milwaukee, 1970, 1971, 1972
Lee College, Cleveland, Tennessee
Micanopy Center of Modern Art, Florida, 1972
"North Carolina Craftsman 1971," Raleigh, North Carolina
North Central Craftsman, Midland, Michigan, 1971
Springfield Museum, Springfield, Illinois, 1971
Winter Park (Florida) Art Festival, 1972

George Thiewes is also represented in the Chrysler Museum of Art, Norfolk, Virginia, and the Smithsonian Institution.

96. George J. Thiewes, United States. 4½". Signed "Thiewes, 1971, Sculptural Landscape, Rainbow, Cloud, Sun"

▶

97. George J. Thiewes, United States. 7¼". Signed "Thiewes, '72, Sculptural Cup"

98. George J. Thiewes, United States. 3½". Signed "Thiewes, Knife"

99.
James M. Wayne, United States. 9″. Signed
"Jim Wayne Gas Glass (series)"

James M. Wayne

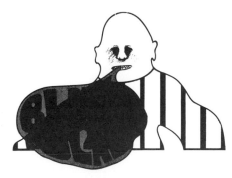

JAMES M. WAYNE ▪ GLASSBLOWER

JAMES M. WAYNE ▪ GLASSBLOWER

JAMES WAYNE

Born in San Francisco, December 28, 1939
Wife: Stephanie Yinger, 1964

With a B.S. from San Jose State College in 1963, James Wayne set out to earn his master's degree with "Blown Glass and Cast Metal Forms" as the subject of his thesis. This he succeeded in doing in 1966. Compositions of blown glass and "lost-wax" cast bronze represent considerable achievements, but carrying the subject into sculptural forms is reaching for the very top in the glass field.

Wayne is one of the leading young glass artists working today. His work is imaginative, with a light, airy quality. (See Color Plate 52.)

During his college years Wayne received a number of scholastic awards and at San Jose was one of the leaders in the arts field. In addition to participating in workshops, he studied with Dominick Labino in 1966 and Paul Soldner in Richmond, California, in 1967. Currently he is associated with his alma mater as instructor of art, after doing similar teaching at the University of Southern California in 1968 and Pasadena City College in 1969.

100.
James M. Wayne, United States. 10½".
Signed "Jim Wayne, U.S.C., 1969"

101.
James M. Wayne, United States. 9½".
Signed "Jim Wayne, 1970, A Lover's Goblet"

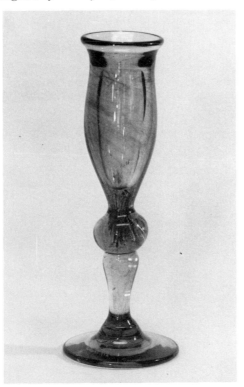

The following list represents some of the permanent collections in which Wayne's work is represented:

Fine Arts Society of San Diego (California)
Mills College, Oakland, California
"Objects U.S.A.," the Johnson Wax Company, Racine, Wisconsin
San Jose State College, San Jose, California
Sheridan College, School of Design, Port Credit, Ontario, Canada
Tacoma (Washington) Art Museum
University of Nebraska, Lincoln, Nebraska
Wichita Art Association, Wichita, Kansas

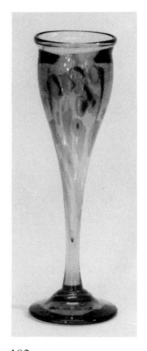

102.
James M. Wayne,
United States. 10½".
Signed "Jim Wayne,
'71"

Wayne's work has appeared in over fifty exhibitions, most of them invitational. The following is a partial list:

Art and Science Center, Nashua, New Hampshire, 1971
Ball State University, Muncie, Indiana, 1967
Berkeley Art Festival, Berkeley, California, 1965
California State Fair, Sacramento, California
Cheney Cowles Museum, Spokane, Washington, 1968
Dallas Museum of Fine Arts, Dallas, Texas, 1967
Long Beach Museum of Art (museum tour), Long Beach, California
John Michael Kohler Arts Center, Sheboygan, Wisconsin
Los Angeles County Art Museum (two-year traveling show)
Lowe Museum of Art, University of Miami, 1965
M. H. DeYoung Memorial Museum, San Francisco, California
Museum of Contemporary Crafts (traveling selection), New York City, 1969
Museum West, San Francisco, California, 1967, 1968
Northern Illinois University, De Kalb, Illinois, 1969
Oregon College of Education, Monmouth, Oregon, 1970
Pasadena Art Museum, Pasadena, California, 1967, 1968
Sacramento Valley Academy of Arts, Carmichael, California, 1971
San Fernando Valley State College Art Department, 1966
Scripps College, Claremont, California, 1968
Toledo Glass Nationals I and II, 1966, 1968
University of Washington, Seattle, Washington, 1968
University of Wisconsin, Wisconsin Union Gallery, Madison, Wisconsin, 1970

ROBERT WILLSON

Robert Willson is a man of multiple skills—painter, decorator, teacher, museum adviser, and glass sculptor. Over the past fifteen years, working for the most part at the factory of Alfredo Barbini in Murano, Italy, he has created some hundred or more glass sculptures. These pieces are well-planned stories in glass art, mostly with internal decoration. There are no limited editions, not even similarities among them— each is a thoughtful expression with beautiful symbols and figurations. (See Color Plates 51, 53, 54, and 55.)

To Willson, the formation of glass is a fine art. His inspiration ranges from the pre-Columbian, Egyptian, or Oriental, to contemporary modern abstracts, and his pieces are named accordingly. Although his work appears on the market only occasionally, the price it commands is a reflection of its quality. If one were to list artists of international scope with great potential for future collectibility, Willson's name would have an important place. His work is not the sort of thing that just any glassman could go to the furnace and create. At present, his production is sporadic, limited by his full-time involvement with the University of Miami Art Department, where he has been since 1952.

Willson earned his B.A. at the University of Texas in 1934. The following year he was given the Farmer International Fellowship to Mexico, and in 1941 he received his M.F.A., with honors, from the University De Bellas Artes there. Willson was honored with a national fellowship to the Corning Museum of Glass in 1956; in 1966/67 he was given a grant for glass studies by the U.S. Department of Education.

Willson's first teaching experience came early in his career—in 1935 at the University of Mexico. From 1940 to 1948, with the exception of the war years, when he was involved in air intelligence, he was head of the art department at Texas

Wesleyan College. He has also been active as a museum director and has helped to found several museums.

Exhibitions of his work have been both national and international—from the Corning Museum of Glass in New York, the Lowe Museum of Art at the University of Miami, and the Ringling Art Museum at Sarasota in Florida to several in Italy. His glass sculptures are in a number of private collections, as well as in the Corning Museum of Glass, the Peoria Art Museum, and the Witte Memorial Museum in this country, and in the Italian National Glass Museum at Murano, the Museo Correr in Venice, and the New Zealand National Art Museum.

The modesty of this talented man belies his influence in the art field. He is deeply committed to his teaching activities and to the goal of good art for all people.

103.
Robert Willson, United States. 22″. Signed "Robert Willson"

104.
Robert Willson, United States. 5¼″. Signed "Robert Willson, Venetian Nude"

CZECHOSLOVAKIA

THE GLASS OF CZECHOSLOVAKIA

Czechoslovakia, known for its beauties of landscape, the interesting architecture of its great cities and towns, and its independent spirit, is today one of the foremost glass producers in the world. Artistic skill, fine workmanship, and the scientific knowledge of the modern Czechoslovak artists follow the great tradition of glassmaking in that country.

The first glassworks originated at about the end of the thirteenth or the beginning of the fourteenth century. Reliable documents provide proof that the oldest glassworks in Central Europe, at Chribska, operated continuously for more that 550 years (from 1414). Further development of the glassworks in the region below the Luzice Mountains proceeded smoothly.

In 1530 a member of the old and renowned Schurer glassmaking family, Pavel, built a glassworks at Falknov, and another glassworks simultaneously originated at Krompach. Additional expansion of glassmaking and more rapid construction of glassworks occurred after the Thirty Years War, when a whole series of factories was built, including one at Novy Zamek in the Ceska Lipa region. This period of expansion was followed by one of relative stagnation caused, in particular, by a lack of wood supplies. It was only at the beginning of the nineteenth century that an experimental direct coal-heating system was introduced when a glassworks was built near Decin.

The next period of extensive glassworks construction in this region took place in the Novy Bor area after 1870. The earliest glassworks in the town of Bor itself was that known as Michlovka, built in 1874, which was followed shortly by several others in the environs—at Skalice, Svor, and Falknov. In 1886 a modern glassworks was built at Kamenicky Senov by Adolf Ruckl. This spate of building activity ended at the beginning of the twentieth century.

The Jilk Glassworks commenced working at Kamenicky Senov in 1905, the Hrdina Glassworks at Prachen in 1907, a training glassworks at Bor in 1910, and the Ladish (later Hantich) Glassworks at Novy Bor in 1913. The period preceding the First World War also saw the foundation of the Rudi Glassworks at Polevsko. Last of this series of glassworks was the Vatter factory at Kamenicky Senov, built in 1925. All the works were provided with gas-generator heating systems. (As a point of interest, it may be noted that the last furnace employing wood as fuel was that at the Nova Glassworks, about 1860.)

In the following decades the glassworks were merely maintained and modernized, the most recent novelty being the introduction—after the Second World War —of a remote gas furnace heating system. In 1945, an annex was built onto the Hantich Glassworks at Novy Bor; there, in the middle of 1965, a modern six-pot top-fired furnace was put into operation. Shortly afterward, on August 20, 1965, construction of a new glassmaking concern was started nearby, at Novy Bor.

The complex of glassworks in this town in the heart of the glassmaking region is thoroughly fascinating. Each factory is equipped with the latest scientific and technical improvements. All the various techniques are used to produce both utilitarian and artistic glass: hand shaping, overlaid decoration, hand sculpturing, and sandblasting. When we visited here and observed the whole operation, we came away tremendously impressed by the capable, efficient manner in which so many beautiful objects were being made. The Novy Bor works are guided by skilled and experienced artists, technicians, and glass masters who continue to foster the extraordinary traditions and achievements of Czechoslovakian glass.

Among other important factories is the Moser Glassworks in Karlovy Vary (Carlsbad), which in 1957 celebrated its one hundredth anniversary. Its founder was Ludwig Moser, whose original trade was glass engraving. He followed in the tradition of the renowned portrait engraver Dominik Biemann, who lived in Karlovy Vary and engraved into glass the portraits of important visitors to the famous spa. Moser, as well as his successors, saw to it that only articles of perfect quality and high artistic value left the glassworks, thereby establishing standards for the creation of a series of characteristic glass sets, well balanced in style and purpose, and also of a series of heavier articles in noteworthy shapes—vases, bowls, jardinieres, dressing-table sets, and so on. Because of the exceptional style and grace of the Moser articles, the list of buyers included numerous noted persons—emperors, kings, maharajahs, diplomats, and foremost artists. Conscientious, superior work has brought the Moser trademark well-deserved fame among glass specialists all over the world, and there is every reason to believe that it will remain highly respected in the future.

Many Czech designers work at their own studios and at the same time cooperate with one or more of the glassworks that, besides domestic glass, produce art glass either on a large scale or in small quantities. The main firms responsible for much of the tremendous volume and variety of art glass production in Czechoslovakia include the Moser works at Karlovy Vary, Bohemia Glassworks at Podebrady, Exbor Glassworks at Novy Bor, Zeleznobrodske at Zelesny Brod, and the Skrdlovice Glassworks.

Zelezny Brod is the region of latest development in the production of glass. The beginning of creative work here goes back to a glassmaking school founded in 1920. Today there are nearly twenty glass artists who actively participate in its

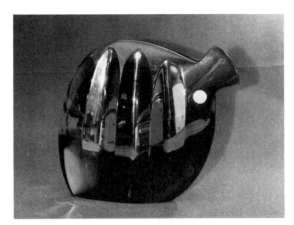

105.
Exbor, Novy Bor, Czechoslovakia. 7″. Signed "Exbor, Czechoslovakia"

106.
Exbor, Novy Bor, Czechoslovakia. 4½″. Signed "Exbor—Fish"

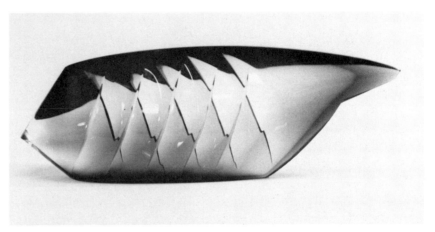

extremely wide range of design, producing glass figurines in sculptured, cut, and engraved patterns. There is also an outstanding group of artists who work in architectural glass of great symbolism and creative originality.

Halfway between Prague and Brno lies the small town of Skrdlovice, which cannot boast of architectural or cultural monuments but is famous for a quite different reason: it possesses a glass factory that produces articles with the highest standards in the world. This factory was founded in 1941 by the glass master Emanuel Beranek, a man of great enterprise. For work in the factory, he acquired local glassmakers from the town and its surroundings who previously had worked in distant factories in the Bohemian-Moravian uplands. Beranek's factory marked the beginning of a new tradition in Skrdlovice—its main concern was not a serial industrial production. On the contrary, every article that left the factory was to be considered a piece of art created by the common effort of artists and glassmakers, who combined their knowledge, experience, skills, and dispositions to achieve it. Such a concept of production has necessitated an equally unusual management; the plant is incorporated in the Centre for Arts and Crafts in Prague, which groups together twenty-eight workshops and ateliers specializing in truly exclusive artistic products.

JAN CERNY

107. Jan Cerny, Czechoslovakia. 3½″. Signed "1971, Jan Cerny, Gnu"

Jan Cerny was born in Rychnov in the Bohemian-Moravian highlands on April 25, 1907. He attended—and was graduated from—the Academy of Applied Arts in Prague, working in the sculptural studio of Professor Josef Maratko. In the years immediately following, he worked as a sculptor and created portraits, plaques, and ornamental pieces using various materials.

Cerny spent more than twenty years as a professor at the glassmaking school at Zelezny Brod, training young people for the extensive Jablonec costume jewelry industry and the Zelezny Brod glassmaking district. He taught drawing and modeling, and fostered in his students individuality in the making and shaping of glass, for which—thanks to his training in a sculptor's studio—he possessed a fine background. For two years he was also a lecturer and instructor in art glass at the School of Applied Arts at Zelezny Brod.

In later years, Cerny has turned from small creations of molten glass for enriching costume jewelry to larger compositions, glass reliefs, and glass sculptures. His works can now be found in many art galleries and museums in Czechoslovakia; among them the East Bohemian Art Salon at Policka, the Museum of the Workman's Movement at Semily, the Museum of Applied Arts in Prague, exhibitions of glass jewelry in Liberec, and also in exhibitions of the Czech book in Stockholm and Moscow. (See Color Plate 56.)

108.
Jan Cerny, Czechoslovakia. 7½″. Signed "Jan Cerny, Danseuse"

109.
Jan Cerny, Czechoslovakia. 12″. Signed "Jan Cerny— 1971, Tulip"

110.
Jan Cerny, Czechoslovakia. 7½″.
Signed "Jan Cerny, 1971, Face"

111.
Jan Cerny, Czechoslovakia. 7½″.
Signed "Jan Cerny, 1971, Bass Player"

112.
Jan Cerny, Czechoslovakia. 4¾″.
Signed "Jan Cerny, Owl"

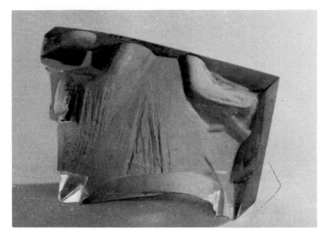

113.
Jan Cerny, Czechoslovakia. 4″. Signed "Jan Cerny, 1971, Bull"

114.
Jan Cerny, Czechoslovakia. 4½″. Signed "Jan Cerny, 1971—Horse"

115–116–117.
Jan Cerny, Czechoslovakia. *(Left)* 4¼″. Signed "Cerny—1971, Bull." *(Center)* 4″. Signed "Jan Cerny, 1971, Fox." *(Right)* 4½″. Signed "Jan Cerny, 1971, Fish."

PAVEL HLAVA

Pavel Hlava, born on June 25, 1924, attended the glassmaking school at Zelezny Brod and the College of Industrial Arts in Prague. From 1948 until 1956 he worked as an independent creative artist, collaborating with the studio of the Czechoslovak army and with the Central Art Studio for glass and ceramic art. From that time to the present, he has worked at the Institute of Interior and Fashion Design in Prague, where he has been involved in all the branches and techniques of glass production, bringing to his work his talent for experimentation and discovery and his keen sense of originality.

Particularly distinguished are Hlava's efforts in the field of offhand-made glass, blown and shaped by the glassmakers directly at the furnace; in cut glass, utility glass, stemware and table sets, pressed glass, and cast glass. His work, outstanding in its originality, is characterized by both orderliness and its powerful expression in both dramatic shapes and colors. It shows the briskness and liveliness of a real innovator, of a searching for new forms and individuality. (See Color Plates 57 and 58.)

118.
Pavel Hlava, Czechoslovakia. 17½″. Signed "P. Hlava, 1966"

119.
Pavel Hlava, Czechoslovakia. 7¾″. Signed "Pavel Hlava, Moser"

120.
Pavel Hlava, Czechoslovakia. 11″. Signed "P. Hlava, Czechoslovakia"

121.
Pavel Hlava, Czechoslovakia. 2¾″. Signed "P. Hlava, Czechoslovakia"

122.
Pavel Hlava, Czechoslovakia. 4″. Signed "P. Hlava, Czechoslovakia"

123.
Pavel Hlava, Czechoslovakia. 19½″. Signed "P. Hlava, Czechoslovakia"

124.
Pavel Hlava, Czechoslovakia. 22½″. Signed "P. Hlava, Czechoslovakia"

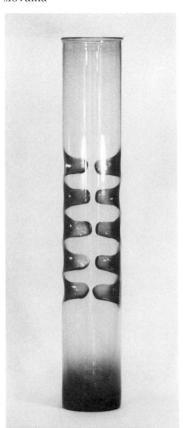

VLADIMIR JELINEK

Vladimir Jelinek was born on February 5, 1934 in the village of Zizice, near Slany in Bohemia. He studied at the Glassmakers Technical School in Kamenicky Senov and at the Academy of Applied Arts in Prague. After completing his studies, he worked as a designer in the Moravian Glassworks; later he cooperated with important institutions concerned with glass production, namely the Centre for Arts and Crafts and the departmental directorate of the Utility Glass Industry, in Novy Bor. Since 1966 he has been working at the Institute of Interior and Fashion Design in Prague.

Vladimir Jelinek concerns himself with plain and decorated tableware (pantograph), cut glass, hollow glass (finished by cutting), glass sculpture, and glass connected with architecture. Lately he has been concentrating on the development of a utility glass to be manufactured by the most modern automatic machines.

Jelinek's work is characterized by sensitivity, modesty, and a sense of proportion. In form it is economical, whether the piece is small and compact or extremely large. The glass objects he designs always appear to be harmonious and to have a kind of simple nobility. (See Color Plate 60.)

125.
Vladimir Jelinek, Czechoslovakia. 6¾″. Signed "V. Jelinek"

126.
Vladimir Jelinek, Czechoslovakia. 8″. Signed "V. Jelinek, 1971"

127.
Vladimir Jelinek, Czechoslovakia. 7½″. Signed "V. Jelinek, 1969"

128.
Vladimir Jelinek, Czechoslovakia. 11¾″. Signed "J. Jelinek, 1972"

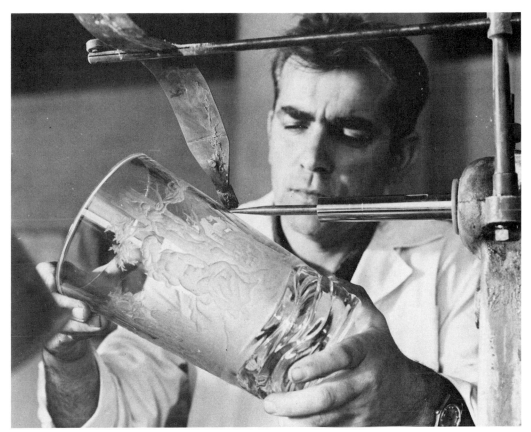

LADISLAV JEZEK

Ladislav Jezek was born on February 9, 1930. He attended the glassmaking school at Zelezny Brod, then finished his education at the College of Industrial Arts in Prague. Since 1957 he has been working at the government enterprise "Zelezno-brodske Sklo" at Zelezny Brod as engraver and glass designer. All his artistic and creative skill are concentrated on the engraving of glass. Especially successful is his collaboration with glass designer Jindrich Tockstein on unique engraved pieces.

Ladislav Jezek has taken part in a number of world exhibitions and salons—for example, the Milan Triennale and the Expo at Brussels. His works excel in delicacy, precision, and artistry, the latest ones being engraved glass blocks, which are featured in Czechoslovak exhibitions. (See Color Plate 65.)

VLADIMIR and ZDENEK KEPKA

Vladimir was born on June 20, 1925, Zdenek on May 4, 1930, at Zlonice. Both learned the profession of their father, who owned a workshop for the production of artistic glass. This profession is traditional in the Kepka family, for it has been passed from father to sons, then to grandsons, even to great-grandsons, since 1847. At present, the Kepka workshop has been incorporated with the Association of Artistic Trades.

Both Kepka brothers have created, without special schooling, works of great artistic merit, particularly sandblasted glass blocks, which are usually decorated with either vivacious figurative motifs or landscape motifs. They showed their creations for the first time in Exhibition Sife in Paris in 1970, and were immediately acclaimed. Currently, they are collaborating with a number of other important and popular Czechoslovak glass designers in the creation of a variety of sandblasted glass windows and other unique objects. (See Color Plate 61.)

Kepka Zdenek

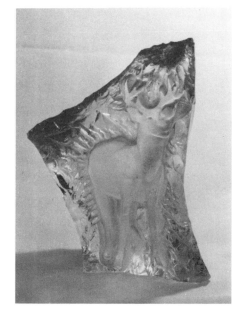

129. Vladimir and Zdenek Kepka, Czechoslovakia. 10″, sandblasted. Signed
"Kepka, 1971, Sitting Woman"

130. Vladimir and Zdenek Kepka, Czechoslovakia. 6½″. Signed "Kepka 14,
Deer"

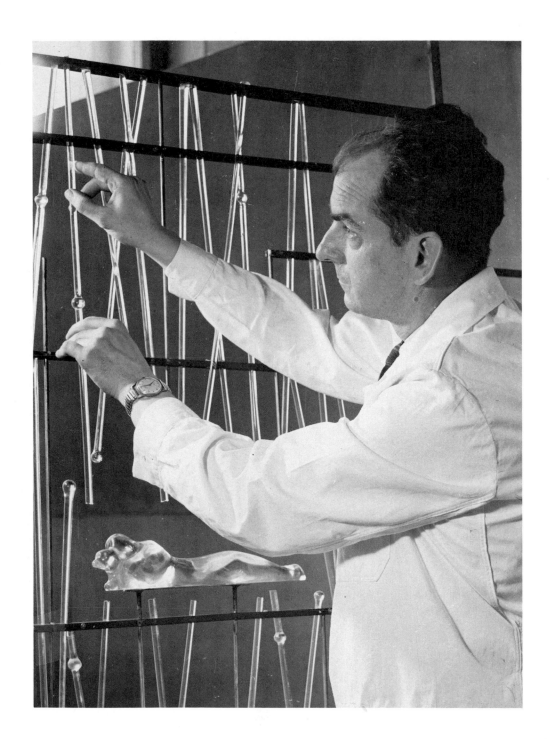

Plate 1.   Michael Boylen, United States. 6 and 6½ inches.

Plate 2.   Jack Brewer, United States. 12¾ and 9¾ inches.

Plate 3.   Donald Carlson, United States. 5¾ and 4½ inches.

Right above

Plate 4.   Bob Biniarz, United States. 4½ and 5 inches.

Plate 5. Boris Dudchenko, United States. 7¼ inches. Signed "Boris Dudchenko"

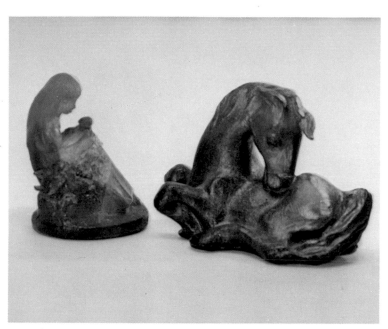

Plate 6. Edris Eckhardt, United States. Both 6½ inches.

Plate 7. Boris Dudchenko, United States. Both 9½ inches. Signed "Boris Dudchenko"

Plate 8. Edris Eckhardt, United States. Tallest, 11¾ inches.

Plate 9. Maurice Heaton, United States. 12 inches. Signed "M.H. 1957/Two Sisters"

Plate 10.   Kent Ipsen, United States. 11 inches.

Plate 11.   Kent Ipsen, United States. 11½ inches. Signed "Kent F. Ipsen, 1972"

Plate 12.   Michael Higgins, United States. 13¼ inches. Signed "Sunset Cruise/Michael Higgins, 1972"

Plate 13.   Michael Higgins, United States. 16 inches. Signed "Michael Higgins, 1972/The War Between"

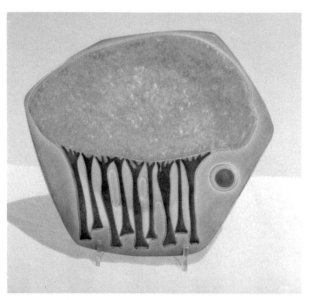

Plate 14.   Frances Higgins, United States. 14 inches. Signed "Frances Higgins, 1971/Multitrunk Tree Platter"

Plate 15.   Michael Higgins, United States. 12½ inches. Signed "Michael Higgins"

Plate 16.   Frances Higgins, United States. 8½ inches. Signed "Frances Higgins, 1969"

Plate 17. Frances Higgins, United States, 15½ inches. Signed "Frances Higgins, 1972/Blue Anemones"

Plate 18. Kent Ipsen, United States. 12 inches. Signed "Kent Ipsen, 1971"

Plate 20. Roland Jahn, United States. 8 and 6¼ inches.

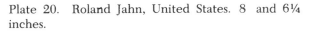

Plate 21. Frank Kulasiewicz, United States. 6 inches. Signed "Kulasiewicz, 1970, Pod"

Plate 22. Frank Kulasiewicz, United States. 6 and 9 inches.

Plate 23.   Dominick Labino, United States. 5¼, 7¾, and 5 inches.

Plate 24.   Dominick Labino, United States. Tallest, 9½ inches.

Plate 25.   Dominick Labino, United States. Piece at **right**, 8 inches.

Plate 26.   Dominick Labino, United States. Piece in center, 9½ inches.

Plate 27.   Dominick Labino, United States. Piece at **right**, 9½ inches.

Plate 28.   Dominick Labino, United States. Piece in center, 5 inches.

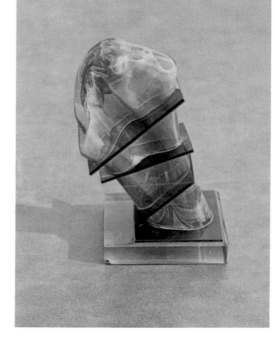

Plate 29.   Dominick Labino, United States. Piece in center, 5½ inches.

Plate 30.   Harvey Littleton, United States. 9 inches. Signed "H. K. Littleton, 1968"

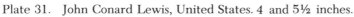

Plate 32.   Harvey Littleton, United States. 8 inches. Signed "Sympathetic Movement/H.K. Littleton, 1968"

Plate 31.   John Conard Lewis, United States. 4 and 5½ inches.

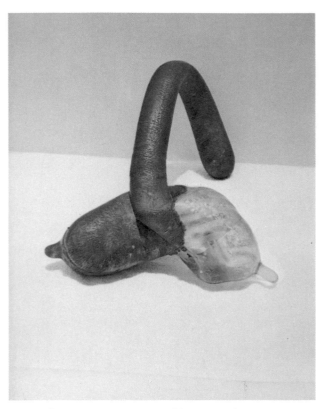

Plate 33. Harvey Littleton, United States. 12¼ inches. Signed "Harvey K. Littleton, 1971"

Plate 34. Marvin Lipofsky, United States. 9¼ inches. Signed "Lipofsky, 1966–67"

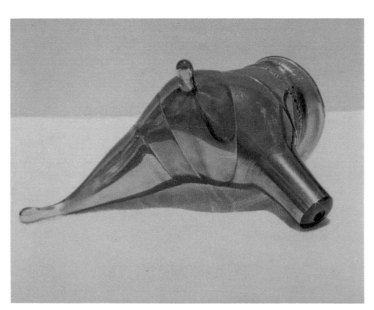

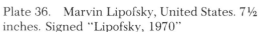

Plate 35. Marvin Lipofsky, United States. 3¾ inches. Signed "Lipofsky, 1966–67"

Plate 36. Marvin Lipofsky, United States. 7½ inches. Signed "Lipofsky, 1970"

MIROSLAV KLINGER

Miroslav Klinger, born January 10, 1922 at Hruba Horka in the Jablonec nad Nisou district, attended the glassmaking school at Zelezny Brod and, like so many others, completed studies at the College of Industrial Arts in Prague. Since 1948 he has been employed at "Zeleznobrodske Sklo" as designer of glass figurines; he has also taught in the glassmaking school at Zelezny Brod, specializing in offhand glass.

Klinger designs utility glass, but his chief activity relates to glass plastics, usually produced by offhand techniques or cut. He handles human and animal themes with keen perception. (See Color Plate 59.)

Professor Klinger won a gold medal at Expo 1958 and the Laureate of State Prize in 1961.

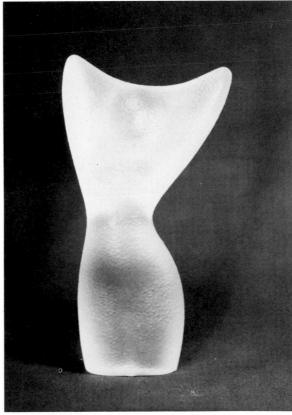

131.
Miroslav Klinger, Czechoslovakia. 9¼". Signed "Klinger, 1971"

132.
Miroslav Klinger, Czechoslovakia. 10¼". Signed "Torso, Klinger"

STANISLAV LIBENSKY and
JAROSLAVA BRYCHTOVA–LIBENSKA

Stanislav Libensky, born March 27, 1921 at Sezemice, near Mnichoro Hradiste, began the study of glass at a relatively early age, becoming acquainted with it at the schools of Novy Bor and Zelezny Brod. After completing his early schooling, he continued his education at the Academy of Applied Arts in Prague. Today he is the ranking professor in the glassmaking studio there, constantly fostering his pupils' enthusiasm for work and inspiring the activities of fellow artists.

A glass painter and artist in one, Libensky attains monumental expressions in glass in the form of colored and etched windows. His freely shaped "bottle objects" are original in design and employ new concepts of painting and overlaying on glass; he achieves a wealth of optical and color shading through inner sculpture. Glass sculptures and windows represent his greatest contribution to the field of Czechoslovakian glass. Because of his methods and ideas, there has been a shift from utilitarianism toward free-form art and unique creations.

Professor Libensky was chairman of the Association of Czechoslovak Creative Artists from 1966 to 1967, and is presently a member of a number of international societies. He has won the Laureate of State Prize Klement Gottwald in his homeland, as well as prizes in Brussels, Belgium, and São Paulo, Brazil.

Jaroslava Brychtova Libenska, the wife of Professor Libensky, was born on July 8, 1921 at Zelezny Brod. She finished the first annual course at the College of Industrial Arts in Prague and also attended the Academy of Plastic Arts. All her time is devoted to the designing of glass. Mrs. Libensky has created, in association with her husband, a large number of plastics and nitrages that embody a new concept of the relationships between glassmaking and sculpture. (See Color Plates 63 and 64.)

133. Stanislav Libensky and Jaroslava Brychtova-Libenska, Czechoslovakia.
8¼". Signed "Libensky-Brychtova, Cubus, 1967"

OLDRICH LIPA

Born in Rychvald, near Ostrava, December 19, 1929

This accomplished glass cutter's studies included the Glassmakers Technical School at Novy Bor, followed by the College of Industrial Arts in Prague. He spent considerable time studying with Professor Kaplicky in his studio.

Oldrich Lipa works as a designer in the Moser Glassworks, Carlsbad Spa, devoting most of his attention to cutting and engraving. However, he also designs utility glass, solitaires, and decorative work. Often he achieves graphic-optical structures by massive vertical and horizontal cuttings, and frequently his vases are embellished with rich engravings in exciting modern conceptions. His solitaires are also distinguished for their beautiful original engraved decoration. (See Color Plate 62.)

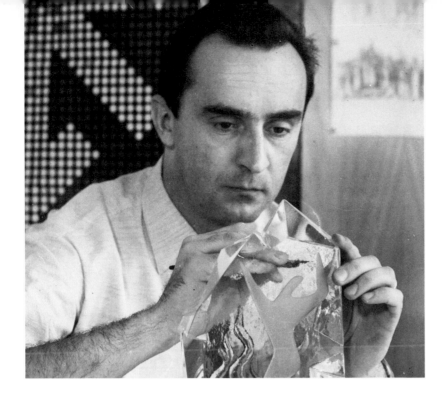

LUBOS METELAK

Lubos Metelak is one of the gifted artists who, by their masterpieces, have influenced Czechoslovak glass production. He was born at Zelezny Brod on March 19, 1934, the son of the respected creative artist, architect Alois Metelak, director of the Arts and Crafts School for the glass industry at Zelezny Brod. After attending this school, Lubos studied at the College of Industrial Arts in Prague. Upon graduation, he became a member of the Association of Czechoslovak Creative Artists.

Since 1962, Metelak has worked as a creative artist and designer at the famous Moser Glassworks in Carlsbad Spa, concentrating mostly on the engraving of glass. His original works, characterized by a very personal style, have been exhibited widely both in Czechoslovakia and abroad. Visitors to the XI Milan Triennale, to the Corning Museum of Glass in 1959, to Moscow, to France and England, to Florence, Italy, and to exhibitions in many other places have had an opportunity to get acquainted with his unusual talents. His glass is also represented in the permanent exhibitions of the Arts and Crafts High School in Prague.

134. Lubos Metalak, Czechoslovakia. 6½". Signed "Moser–1970–Metalak"

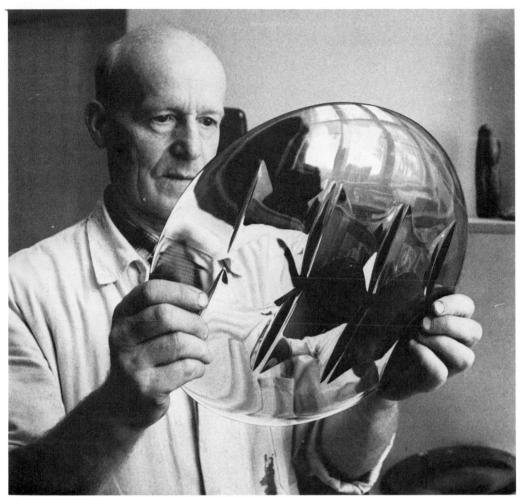

BRATISLAV NOVAK

Bratislav Novak was born on January 21, 1913, at Kostalov, near Semily. He studied at the glassmaking school at Zelezny Brod, and now is a teacher in that school, specializing in cut glass, mainly pieces such as vases, dishes, and figurines finished on polishing machines. His aim is a rich optical effect, which he secures by bulky, smooth-polished planes, often in combination with well-defined base lines. Novak also makes use of an infinitude of rotary movements by means of horizontal cuttings. (See Color Plate 69.)

RENE ROUBICEK

Professor Rene Roubicek, born January 21, 1922, in Prague, studied at the College of Industrial Arts there. Since 1945 he has been working at Novy Bor, first as professor in the glassmaking school at Kamenicky Senov, and since 1952 as a leading glass designer. But he has remained interested in educational work, with special attention to the glass branch of the Academy of Art in Prague.

Professor Roubicek is a poet in glass. Guided by a strong power of invention, he has the ability to make complicated shapes that enhance the optical qualities, brilliance, and rich color of glass. His many experiments have been concentrated on researching optical effects through unusual dramatic creations. In 1967 he won the coveted honor of Laurea of State in his homeland, and he is the holder of many other prizes both at home and abroad. (See Color Plate 66.)

135.
Rene Roubicek, Czechoslovakia. 20″.
Signed "Roubicek, 1971"

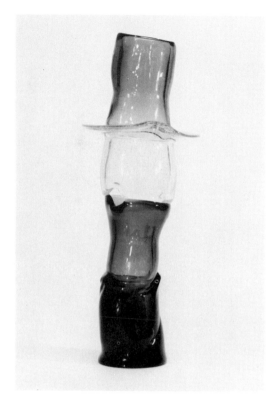

136.
Rene Roubicek, Czechoslovakia. 20″. Signed "Roubicek, 1971"

137.
Rene Roubicek, Czechoslovakia. 13½″. Signed "Roubicek, 1965"

138.
Rene Roubicek, Czechoslovakia. 11½″. Signed "Roubicek, 1970"

139.
Rene Roubicek, Czechoslovakia. 7½″. Signed "Roubicek, 1965"

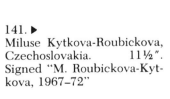

MILUSE KYTKOVA-ROUBICKOVA

Miluse Kytkova-Roubickova, the wife of Rene Roubicek, was born in Prague on July 20, 1922, and completed her university studies at the Academy of Applied Arts there. She designed, for the Council of Industrial Design in Prague, a wide range of outstanding creations using varied techniques and creative concepts. Her replicas of natural shapes, fruits, and flowers are particularly well known. Visitors to the Montreal, Canada, and Osaka, Japan, World's Fairs had the opportunity of seeing her delightful creations. (See Color Plate 67.)

140.
Miluse Kytkova-Roubickova, Czechoslovakia. 18". Signed "M. Roubickova, 1971, Glass Bouquet"

141. ▶
Miluse Kytkova-Roubickova, Czechoslovakia. 11½". Signed "M. Roubickova-Kytkova, 1967–72"

142.
Miluse Kytkova-Roubickova, Czechoslovakia. 12″.
Signed "M. Roubickova-Kytkova, 1972"

143.
Miluse Kytkova-Roubickova, Czechoslovakia. 11¼″. Signed "M. Roubickova, 1968"

144.
Miluse Kytkova-Roubickova, Czechoslovakia. 12¼″. Signed "M. Roubickova-Kytkova, 1967–72"

145.
Miluse Kytkova-Roubickova, Czechoslovakia. 10″. Signed "M. Roubickova-Kytkova, 1967"

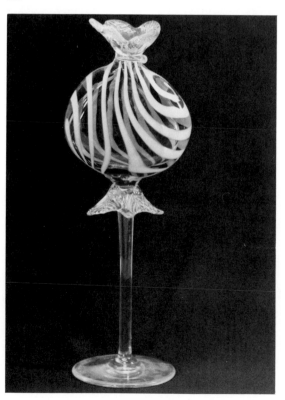

DR. JAROMIR SPACEK

Born on May 15, 1911, at Drevnovice in the Prostejov district. Jaromir Spacek finish his secondary school studies at Prostejov, then went to the university at Brno, where he earned the degree of doctor of natural sciences. Since 1936, with the exception of the World War II years, he has been headmaster of the Glassmakers Technical School at Novy Bor and, during some of that period (1957 to 1961), principal of the Glassmakers Technical School at Kamenicky Senov. Besides organizational activities connected with the management of the schools, he has endeavored to find new ways of handling offhand techniques as these relate to the decoration of glass. In the process, he developed thirteen patented methods of manufacture. He has also occupied himself with creative problems.

Some of Dr. Spacek's patents have been bought by the various Czech glass-works. "Bor glass" received a gold medal for a work by Pavel Hlava that was manufactured according to one of the methods patented by Spacek. All his patents are aimed at decorating glass directly at the glass oven; they require a high grade of technological knowledge and skill.

The exhibition of glass at the Novy Bor Glass Museum is a culmination of Dr. Spacek's outstanding discoveries and experiments. Here are displayed pieces showing the purity of shape and natural feeling of the work of this outstanding artist. (See Color Plate 68.)

146. Dr. Jaromir Spacek, Czechoslovakia. 11¼". Signed "Dr. Spacek, 1964, Bureaucrat"

147.
Dr. Jaromir Spacek, Czechoslovakia. 10″.
Signed "Dr. Spacek, 1969, Notre Dame"

148.
Dr. Jaromir Spacek, Czechoslovakia. 4½″.
Signed "Dr. Spacek, 1969, Cosmic Odys-
seus"

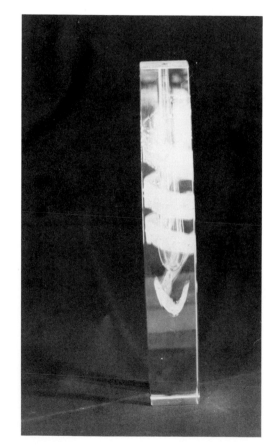

149.
Dr. Jaromir Spacek, Czechoslovakia. 8¾″.
Signed "Dr. Spacek, 1968, Adam and Eve"

150.
Dr. Jaromir Spacek, Czechoslovakia. 12¼″.
Signed "Dr. Spacek, 1961"

JINDRICH TOCKSTEIN

Tockstein was born on July 14, 1914. He studied at the glassmaking school at Zelezny Brod and then at the College of Industrial Arts in Prague. Currently he is working as a creative artist in "Zeleznobrodske Sklo," specializing in engraving and also contributing his skills to rich figurative compositions that transfer a profound human theme to glass planes or blocks. He makes use of stylistic drawings both figurative and abstract. (See Color Plate 73.)

151.
Jindrich Tockstein, Czechoslovakia. 5¾". Signed "Tockstein-Frohlich, Girls, 1970"

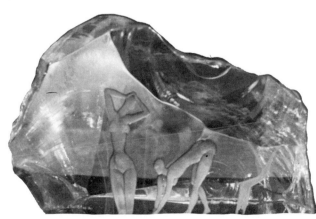

DENMARK

KASTRUP AND HOLMEGAARD GLASSWORKS

Production of glassware has never come naturally to the country of Denmark since it is without the essential raw materials, particularly fuel. The first glassworks was nevertheless built about 1550 at Mariager Fiord in Jutland, and in the period before 1650 a long row of small glassworks was constructed. After that year, however, the production of glass in Denmark ceased, mainly on account on the shortage of fuel.

About a century later, in the decade between 1740 and 1750, the first glassworks in the Scandinavian peninsula was built in the endless forests that covered Sweden and Norway. At that time Denmark and Norway were one realm reigned over by one king, and it was therefore natural for Denmark to patronize the Norwegian glassworks, which actually monopolized the sale of glassware to Denmark. But, as a result of the Napoleonic Wars, Norway was separated from Denmark and entered into union with Sweden. (It did not become an independent kingdom until 1905.)

For Denmark the early years of the nineteenth century were troublesome ones. Great efforts were made to promote trade and improve economic affairs in order to put the country on a sound footing. Such was the situation when the owners of the great Holmegaard's Moor, about seven kilometers north of Naestved in the southern part of the island of Zealand, first thought of exploiting the great quantities of peat in the moor as fuel for a glass industry, partly because there was then no glassworks in Denmark and partly because glassmaking was one of the most fuel-consuming trades. Since, for more than 200 years, glass had not been produced in Denmark proper, there were many problems to be solved. For one thing, there were no glassblowers, so a glassblower named Wendt and his two sons were brought from Norway. It was they who erected the first glass furnace at Holmegaard's Moor. Work began November 5, 1825.

Count Christian Danneskiold-Samsøe, who had fathered the idea of a glassworks, unfortunately died before the enterprise was inaugurated. It fell to his widow, Henriette Danneskiold-Samsøe, to continue the work and become the actual founder of the glass industry in modern Denmark. Ever since then, glass has been produced in this very same place.

The factory was named Holmegaard after the Manor of Holmegaard on the land where it was situated, and after the moors from which peat was extracted for fuel for almost exactly 100 years. Peat is usable fuel if sufficiently dry, but wet summers often created difficulties, holding up the production. Nevertheless, the results exceeded the expectations, and the glassmaking activity continued to grow.

The first production consisted solely of inexpensive green bottles, the so-called bouteilles. Ten years later, in 1835, the production of service glass was taken up. As the first imported Norwegian glassblowers did not master this line of production, glassblowers were brought from Bohemia and southern Germany, and they formed the nucleus of the great staff of glassblowers from which the Danish glass industry is descended today.

In 1847 other glassworks were built, the first one at Kastrup, near the coast of Copenhagen, close to the present airport, and the production of green bottles was then carried on there in the closest possible vicinity to the important Copenhagen market, while the production of service glass went on at Holmegaard's. The two enterprises had the same management until 1873, when Count Danneskiold-Sams øe sold Kastrup Glasvaerk to a joint-stock company, which soon took over a number of other glassworks.

Holmegaard was not alone in producing service glass. In 1834 a glass factory, Conradsminde, was established south of Alborg in Jutland. Even these works were situated near a moor, but they preferred wood for fuel. This factory existed until 1857. Its products are extremely rare today, and in great demand; they have a certain robust charm. A few specimens of these Jutland glasses with their remarkable cobalt tint can still be seen at the Alborg Museum of History, but the output was small and not marketed beyond northern Jutland.

When Conradsminde closed down, production in Jutland was carried on by a glassworks newly built at Alborg in 1852, which manufactured a range of service glass and glassware for industrial purpose until 1925.

Still other Danish towns also set up their own glassworks, among them Arhus and Odense. All these works, except Holmegaard, were merged in 1907 into the Kastrup Glasvaerk, which in this way came to control the total production of industrial glassware. In 1912 the first fully automatic bottle-blowing machine was introduced. This soon resulted in the closing of the small bottle factories.

During this time Holmegaard carried on, completely dominating the production of service glass. It made all the ordinary popular service sets and offered all the types of decoration used at the time, such as grinding, engraving, painting, and so on. In 1880 the crystal type or chink glasses were introduced; about 1910 came the modern cracked-off wineglasses, an important development.

In 1924 a close cooperation was inaugurated with the Royal Danish Porcelain Factory, for the purpose of designing service sets to match the sets of the porcelain. This development led to the employment of Holmegaard's first artist, Orla Juul Nielsen, later succeeded by the architect Jacob E. Bang, who more than any other individual contributed to the creation of a modern Danish glass art in the years around 1930. The work of Jacob Bang was continued by Per Lutken; since 1942 he has been Holmegaard's leading artist. (After some years in the ceramic trade, Jacob Bang returned to the glass craft in 1957, in the employ of Kastrup Glasvaerk, where he worked until his death in 1965.)

Following the closing of some of the bottle factories during the 1920s, Kastrup Glasvaerk had only three factories left. These were the original plant at Kastrup, with a production mainly of industrial glassware but with one furnace left for handmade service glasses; a factory at Hellerup close to the Tuborg Breweries, which produced beer bottles; and one factory at Odense that specialized in lighting accessories and household glassware.

It should also be mentioned that as early as the 1880s Kastrup had been the first in Denmark to produce pressed glass. After the engagement of Jacob Bang, this line was extended with a series of glasswares, particularly at the Odense plant.

At length Holmegaard took up the production of industrial glassware, installing the first fully automatic machinery in 1935. Since then this production has rapidly increased.

The Danish glass production was still far from sufficient to cover the needs of the home market. Both glassworks had, nonetheless, built up an extensive export of handmade glasses in spite of the growing competition abroad, especially from countries that had a considerably lower wage level. To meet this competition with a united front against the many industrial mergers taking place in Europe, the boards of directors of the two glassworks, representing together the total Danish production of service and industrial glassware, decided in July 1965 to merge the two companies under the joint name of Kastrup og Holmegaard Glasvaerker A/S.

After a period of separation lasting almost 100 years, the two concerns, both founded by the Danneskiold-Samsøe family, have now joined forces. Together, the four factories and the head office in Copenhagen, in Nerre Veldgade, employ about 1,700 persons. The day-to-day production consists of 15,000 handmade glasses and about one million industrial glasses. Almost 25 percent of the production of handmade glassware is now exported all over the world, frequently hand in hand with the Danish silver and Danish porcelain.

HOLME GAARD
OF COPENHAGEN

BY APPOINTMENT TO
THE ROYAL DANISH COURT

PER LUTKEN

Per Lutken, born in 1916, was educated at the Danish School of Arts, Crafts, and Industrial Design in Copenhagen, under the direction of Jens Moller-Jensen. Lutken graduated in 1937. In 1942, he was employed by Holmegaard Glassworks A/S, and he is still their chief artist today.

Lutken has been represented in all the official Danish artware exhibitions for twenty-seven years, and has participated in numerous other shows, such as Design in Scandinavia, U.S.A., 1954–57; Newe Form aus Danemark, Germany, 1956–57; Formes Scandinaves, Paris, 1958; and The Arts of Denmark, U.S.A., 1960–62. He was the organizer of the exhibition "The Drinking Glass" at Louisiana (museum) in Humlebaek, Denmark, in 1963. (See Color Plate 70.)

Lutken's work is part of the permanent exhibitions or has been shown at the following places, among others:

Corning Museum of Glass, Corning, New York
Das Danische Institute, Dortmund, West Germany
Die Stadtische Gallerie, Oberhausen, West Germany
Formsammlung der Stadt Braunschweig, West Germany
Heue Sammlung, Munich, West Germany
House of Denmark, San Diego, California

Landes Gewerbe Museum, Stuttgart, West Germany

Louisiana, Humlebaek, Denmark

Musée du Verre, Liège, Belgium

Museum of Applied Art, Copenhagen, Denmark

Museum fur Kunst und Gewerbe, Hamburg, West Germany

Museum Haaretz, Tel Aviv, Israel

The Triennale, Milan, Italy

Victoria and Albert Museum, London, England

152.
Per Lutken, Denmark. 8¼". Signed "R1970, Holmegaard, 2356, Per Lutken"

153.
Per Lutken, Denmark. 5¾". Signed "Holmegaard 2342, Per Lutken"

◄154.
Per Lutken, Denmark. 6½". Signed "Per Lutken, R1970, Holmegaard 2398"

155.
Per Lutken, Denmark. 6". Signed "R1970, Holmegaard 2275, Per Lutken"

156.
Per Lutken, Denmark. 7¾″. Signed "R1970, Holmegaard 2363, Per Lutken"

157.
Per Lutken, Denmark. 4½″. Signed "R1970, Holmegaard 2394, Per Lutken"

158.
Per Lutken, Denmark. 9″. Signed "R1970, Per Lutken, Holmegaard 2396"

159.
Per Lutken, Denmark. 14¼″. Signed "R1970, Per Lutken, Holmegaard 2382"

ENGLAND

DILLON CLARKE

Dillon Clarke (signature)

Born in Sandbach, Cheshire, England, February 18, 1946
Married to historian Peter F. Clarke

This fine young artist entered Stoke-on-Trent College of Art in 1962, and in her second year received the prize for sculpture, an award for painting, and the Booth-royd Award. Transferring to Hornsey College of Art in London, after three years there she gained a place at the Royal College of Art—in the School of Ceramics and Glass, under the tutelage of Professor Lord Queensberry and Samuel J. Herman, where she acquired her M.S. degree in art.

Upon graduation from the Royal College of Art, she continued working in glass at The Glasshouse, founded by Sam Herman in 1969 at Covent Garden. Then she became a lecturer at High Wycombe College of Technology and Art in Bucking-hamshire, where she built a glassblowing furnace and set up a department of glass in the School of Design and Furniture.

When working with glass, Mrs. Clarke seems most interested in controlling the fluid nature of the metal. Her sculptural work is light in feeling and excitingly colorful. (See Color Plate 74.)

160. Dillon Clarke, England. 12¼″. Signed "Dillon—May 1970, London"

In addition to being featured in numerous magazine articles, Mrs. Clarke's work—in the brief period of only three years—has appeared in many exhibitions, including the following:

Portsmouth Art Gallery and Museum, 1969
"British Week," Finland, 1970
The Craft Centre of Great Britain, "End and Beginning," 1970
Farnley Hall Arts Centre Festival, 1970
Victoria and Albert Museum, London, 1970–71
Camden Arts Center, London, 1971
Museum of South Australia
The Gardner Centre, Sussex University, 1971
Liberty's Glass Department, opening exhibition, 1971
Society of Craftsmen, Hereford, Wales, 1971

JOHN HEALD COOK

Born in Chorley, Lancashire, September 19, 1942

As a full-time teacher of glassmaking and design at Leicester Polytechnic, John Cook now has the opportunity to make use of his talents in the field of artistic glass. Sculptural forms based on fanciful ideas seem to be one of his identifications, as was evidenced by the specimens of his work shown at Expo '70 in Osaka, Japan.

After studying product design at Leeds College of Art, where he gained a N.D.D. (1962–65), Cook studied glass at the Royal College of Art from 1965 to 1968 and earned an M.Des. degree. During this period he also studied glass design at the Academy of Applied Arts in Prague, and in 1968 he did considerable traveling on the Continent on a scholarship, becoming a visiting designer at the fine Venini Glassworks in Murano, Italy.

Returning to England in 1969, Cook set up a small but quickly developing glassworks at Leicester Polytechnic. His works are in the Victoria and Albert Museum in London, the Corning Museum of Glass, and in numerous other museums as well as traveling exhibitions. (See Color Plates 71 and 72.)

161. John H. Cook, England. 9½". Signed "John H. Cook, London, 1970, Exhibited Expo '70, Osaka, Japan"

John H. Cook.

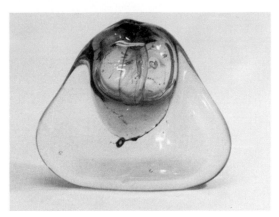

162. John H. Cook, England. 4¾". Signed "John H. Cook, London, 1968"

▶

163. John H. Cook, England. 8¼". Signed "John H. Cook, 1971"

164. John H. Cook, England. 4". Signed "John H. Cook, London, 1968, Exhibited Expo '70, Osaka"

KEITH RICHARD CUMMINGS

Born in London, July 15, 1940

Since 1967 Keith Cummings has been a lecturer in glass at Stourbridge College of Art, Stourbridge, England, specializing in flat glass techniques, in sculptural and architectural approaches for the individual. His work has been influenced by his investigations into the behavior of blown and cast glass when constrained by molds he has devised and made. The result has been interesting and appealing sculptures in glass.

Cummings attended Alleyns College, University of Durham, and Kings College, graduating in 1962 with a B.A. degree. After studying painting under Victor Pasmore and stained glass under Leonard Evetts, he went to work for Whitefriars

165.
Keith Cummings, England. 10″. Signed
"Keith Cummings, 1970"

Glass Company in 1963/64 as an experimental designer for new forms of architectural glass, and developed several techniques for them, including fused glass and architectural slabs. While at Whitefriars he also designed a number of special architectural features, including fused glass screens for the United Glass Building. It would undoubtedly be correct to say that when Keith Cummings has more time to devote to his own glassmaking, he will enjoy an enviable position as a glass sculptor because his pieces to date have been unusual and original in concept. (See Color Plate 75.)

166.
Keith Cummings, England. 10¼″. Signed "Keith Cummings, 1970"

167.
Keith Cummings, England. 4″. Signed "Keith Cummings"

◀168.
Keith Cummings, England. 6¾″. Signed "Keith Cummings, 1970"

169.
Keith Cummings, England. 5″. Signed "Keith Cummings, 1970"

SAMUEL J. HERMAN

Born in Mexico City, 1936

At the age of nine Sam Herman moved with his family to the United States, and from 1955 to 1959 he served in the United States Navy. His education includes a B.A. degree from Western Washington State College in 1962, an M.S. from the University of Wisconsin in 1965; then further studies at Edinburgh College of Art, Scotland, 1965/66, and the Royal College of Art, London, 1966/67. He received scholarships and fellowships from the University of Wisconsin, Haystack School of Crafts, a Fulbright grant, and a Research Fellowship from the Royal College of Art. At present he is the senior tutor in charge of the glass department of the School of Ceramics and Glass, Royal College of Art, London.

It would be difficult to overestimate the impact of Sam Herman in the field of English studio glass today. In addition to the beautiful work in the style of the Art Nouveau period that he has personally done, Herman has designed a remarkably successful line of glass in his own style for the Val St. Lambert factory, which their glassmen are producing from his experimental models. Sam Herman is certainly one of the best-known glass artists in England—if not *the* best best known—and he is quickly achieving an equal position in Europe. An extremely competent lecturer, he has been an asset at the glass workshops he has attended. There is little question but that in the years to come, with his style and the quantity of individual and unique work he does, he will be at the top of the list along with a number of other remarkable artists of today whose work is destined to be greatly sought after. (See Color Plates 76, 77, 79, and 80.)

Herman's work is in the following collections:

170. Samuel J. Herman, England. 10½". Signed "Samuel J. Herman, 1971"

Corning Museum of Glass, Corning, New York
Derby Museum and Art Gallery, Derby, England
Glass Museum, Dusseldorf, West Germany
Gulbenkian Museum, Lisbon, Portugal
Kunstindustrimuseet, Oslo, Norway
Leicester Museum and Art Gallery, Leicester, England
London Country Council, London, England
Musée de Verre de Charleroi, France
Museum of Glass and Jewelry, Jablonec, Czechoslovakia
Palais Stoclet, Brussels, Belgium
Rohnska Konstslojdmuseet, Gothenburg, Sweden
Royal Family of Belgium
Royal Scottish Museum, Edinburgh
University of Wisconsin, Madison, Wisconsin
Victoria and Albert Museum, London

Between 1967 and 1971, Herman's work has appeared in countless shows, including exhibitions at the following:

Primavera Gallery, London, 1967, 1969
Bottcherstrasse, Bremen, 1968
P.U.B., Stockholm, 1968
Boymans-Van Beuningen, Museum, Rotterdam, 1969
Craft Centre of Great Britain, London, 1969
Gemeentemuseum, Arnhem, The Netherlands, 1969
Groningen Museum, Groningen, The Netherlands, 1969
Seibu (store), Tokyo, 1969
Gallery Lecuyer, Brussels, 1970
Camden Arts Centre, London, 1971
Pilkington Museum, St. Helens, Lancashire, England, 1971

171.
Samuel J. Herman, England. 7¼". Signed "Samuel J. Herman, 1969"

172.
Samuel J. Herman, England. 8½″.
Signed "Samuel J. Herman, 1971"

173.▶
Samuel J. Herman, England. 15″. Signed
"Samuel J. Herman, 1971"

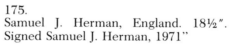

◀174.
Samuel J. Herman, England. 7¼″.
Signed "Samuel J. Herman"

175.
Samuel J. Herman, England. 18½″.
Signed Samuel J. Herman, 1971"

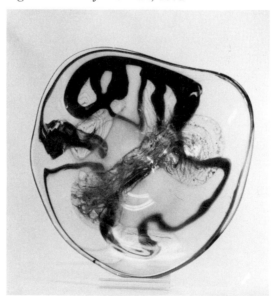

◀176.
Samuel J. Herman, England. 8¾″.
Signed "Samuel J. Herman, 1971"

177.
Samuel J. Herman, England. 10″. Signed
"Samuel J. Herman, 1970"

178.
Samuel J. Herman, England. 9½″.
Signed "Samuel J. Herman, 1971"

179. ▶
Samuel J. Herman, England. 7½″.
Signed "Samuel J. Herman, 1971"

180.
Samuel J. Herman, England. 7″. Signed
"Samuel J. Herman, 1970"

181.
Samuel J. Herman, England. 7½″.
Signed "Samuel J. Herman, 1971"

182.
Samuel J. Herman, England. 6¾″.
Signed "Samuel J. Herman, 1971"

183.
Samuel J. Herman, England. 6¾″.
Signed "Samuel J. Herman, 1970"

PAULINE M. SOLVEN

Born in England, June 28, 1943
Married to Harry Cowdy, film director for BBC Television, 1971

Stourbridge College of Art, from 1961 to 1965, provided this accomplished artist her first opportunity to study at the college level in a glass department with furnaces. Here Pauline Solven designed first, and then blew, her own sculptural pieces. (At this time it was thought impossible for an artist-designer to make his own glass. In England, the only way to become a skilled glassblower was to be apprenticed to a master-craftsman in a factory for several years.) For the following three years, Miss Solven was at the Royal College of Art, London, where—under the tutelage of Sam Herman—a small low-cost furnace developed in the United States was set up. This enabled her to start blowing her own glass professionally.

After leaving the Royal College of Art, Pauline Solven spent a year working at the glass studio of Asa Brandt, Torshalla, Sweden, was one of the first people to work in an independent glass studio in Europe. On returning to England, Miss Solven helped in setting up The Glasshouse, Covent Garden, London, which she managed for a year and where she also produced glass. The Glasshouse was the first place in England where artists in glass could use the facilities and the public could watch and buy. Growing things, such as flowers, trees, grass, and fungi, are the basis of her design inspirations, and the lightness of her compositions fully attests to her ability to handle glass in these sculptural forms. (See Color Plate 78.)

An impressive list of exhibitions indicates her talent:

"British Week," Helsinki, Finland, 1970
"British Week," Stockholm, Sweden, 1968

Building Centre, Birmingham, England, 1965
Camden Arts Centre, London, 1970
Corning Glass Museum, Corning, New York, 1968
Crafts Centre of Great Britain, London, 1968
Expo '70, Osaka, Japan, 1970
Form Design Centre, Malmo, Sweden, 1969
Glass Manufacturers' Federation, London, 1965
Seibu (store), Tokyo, Japan, 1969
Sussex University, England, 1970

184.
Pauline Solven, England. 5½". Signed "Pauline Solven, 1971"

185.
Pauline Solven, England. 8½". Signed "Pauline Solven, 1971"

Plate 37. Jim Lundberg, United States. Pieces at the ends, 6¼ inches.

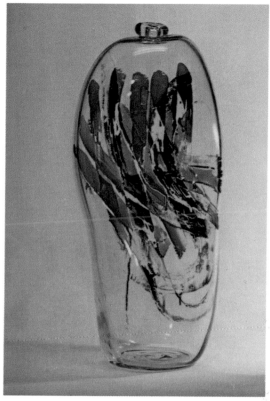

Plate 38.   Joel Philip Myers, United States. 17 inches.

Plate 39.   Steven Mildwoff, United States. 4¾ and 7¼ inches.

Plate 40.   Charles Lotton, United States. Piece in center, 4¼ inches.

Plate 41. Joel Philip Myers, United States. 13 inches.

Plate 42. Joel Philip Myers, United States. 10 and 9 inches.

Plate 43. Robert E. Naess, United States. Piece in center, 3 inches.

Plate 44. Robert E. Naess, United States. 5¼ inches. Signed "R. Naess, 1969/Foetus Charm"

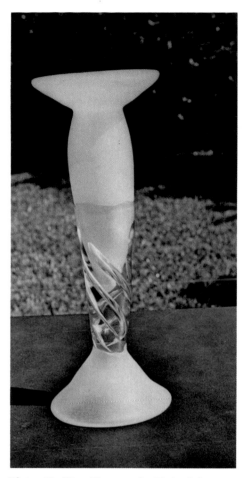

Plate 46. Mark Peiser, United States. Signed "Mark Peiser 1971"

Plate 45. Kim Newcomb, United States. 14 inches. Signed "Newcomb, 1971"

Plate 47. Mark Peiser, United States. 8½ and 8 inches.

Plate 48. Jack A. Schmidt, United States. Taller piece, 11 inches.

Plate 49. George J. Thiewes, United States. Piece in center, 4¾ inches.

Plate 50. James L. Tanner, United States. Piece in center, 4¾ inches.

Plate 51. Robert Willson, United States. 9 inches. Signed "Robert Willson, Static Moon Dance"

Plate 52. James M. Wayne, United States. Piece in center, 7¼ inches.

Plate 53. Robert Willson, United States. 16 inches. Signed "Robert Willson, Italia"

Plate 54. Robert Willson, United States. 15¼ inches. Signed "Robert Wilson, Italia, Stone Letter"

Plate 55. Robert Willson, United States. 10 inches. Signed "Robert Willson, Italy, 1968"

Plate 56. Jan Cerny, Czechoslovakia. 7½ inches. Signed "Jan Cerny, 1971/Two Faces"

Plate 57. Pavel Hlava, Czechoslovakia. 21½ inches. Signed "P. Hlava, 1968"

Plate 58. Pavel Hlava, Czechoslovakia. 18 inches. Signed "P. Hlava, Czechoslovakia"

Plate 59. Miroslav Klinger, Czechoslovakia. 17¼ inches.

Plate 60. Vladimir Jelinek, Czechoslovakia. 9¼ inches. Signed "V. Jelinek, 1970, #U1861/X561–Moser"

Plate 61. Kepka, Czechoslovakia. 20¾ inches.

Plate 62. Oldrich Lipa, Czechoslovakia. 13½ inches

Plate 63. Stanislav Libensky, Czechoslovakia. 14½ inches. Signed "Libensky-Brychtova/ Head–'56"

Plate 64. Stanislav Libensky, Czechoslovakia. 6 inches.

Plate 65. Ladislav Jezek, Czechoslovakia. 6½ inches. Signed "L. Jezek-Mencl, 1970, 'Family'"

Plate 66. Rene Roubicek, Czechoslovakia. 15¼ inches. Signed "Roubicek, 1971"

Plate 67. Miluse Kytkova Roubickova, Czechoslovakia. 11½ inches. Signed "M. Roubickova-Kytkova, 1972"

Plate 68. Dr. Jaromir Spacek, Czechoslovakia. Piece in center, 5 inches.

Plate 69. Bratislav Novak, Czechoslovakia. 7¾ and 4¼ inches.

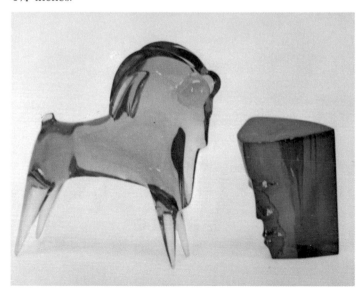

FINLAND

186.
Tapio Wirkkala, Finland. 8″. Signed "Wirkkala"

ITTALA GLASSWORKS

Iittala was founded in 1881. Karhula, which came into being in 1888, eventually transferred its art and table-glass section to Iittala—the two firms came under the same ownership. After Iittala was modernized in 1945, it became one of the most prominent glass companies in the world. Fine designers, such as Tapio Wirkkala in 1947 and Timo Sarpaneva, have been employed by the company. Sarpaneva, whose glass panel "Ice Pack" was shown at the Finnish exhibit at Expo '67, is unquestionably one of the great glass artists of today, as well as an outstanding designer in other mediums.

TIMO SARPANEVA

Born in Helsinki, 1926

Timo Sarpaneva is a Finnish designer with achievements in many fields. Since 1949 he has aroused great admiration for his art glass, which is noted for its pure lines and technical perfection. His other fields of work include utility glassware, lamps, wallpaper design, color scales, typography, door handles, cast iron utensils, and textiles. In addition to personal contributions in these categories, Sarpaneva is a teacher at the Industrial Art Institute, where students eagerly seek him out.

His far-ranging activities have brought him many appointments and honors: Honorary Royal Designer of the Royal Society of Arts, London, 1964, 1967; member of the Stately Committee of Design; member of the board of the Institute of Industrial Design; art director at AB Kinnasand (textile mill), Sweden, and the Porin Puuvilla Oy (cotton mill) 1955–66; consultant on export design in Iceland, 1970. He has been the designer for seven industrial operations in all, in as many fields. In 1958, the Brazilian government invited him there for lectures and exhibits of Finnish arts and crafts.

Fifteen prize awards attest to the quality of his work, among them: three Grand Prix in the Milan Triennales, the Lunning Prize (1956) to the best designer in the Scandinavian countries, and three first prizes (1956) at the exhibition "Young Scandinavians" in the United States. In fact, he has participated in exhibitions in an impressive list of countries:

Exhibition of Finnish Arts and Crafts, Tokyo, 1967
Expo '67, Finnish Section, Montreal, Canada
Grand Palais, Paris, 1963
"H–55," Halsingborg, Sweden, 1955
Kunstgewerbemuseum, Zurich
Stedelijk Museum, Amsterdam
Victoria and Albert Museum, London, 1962

Sarpaneva's works can be seen in the following museums:

Konstindustrimuseum, Copenhagen
Konstindustrimuseum, Stockholm
Louisiana, Humlebaek, Denmark
Malmo Museum, Malmo, Sweden
Museum of Modern Art, New York
Nationalmuseum, Stockholm
Neue Sammlung, Munich, West Germany
Nordfjeldske Kunstindustrimuseot, Trondheim, Norway
Rohnska Konstslojdmuseet, Gothenburg, Sweden
Sammlung der Stadt Braunschweig, West Germany
Stedelijk Museum, Amsterdam, The Netherlands
Victoria and Albert Museum, London

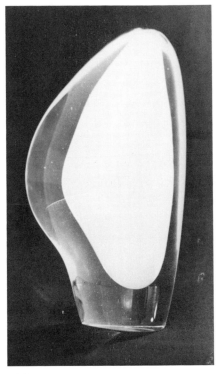

187.
Timo Sarpaneva, Finland.
9¾″. Signed "Sarpaneva,
Lancet"

RIIHIMAEN LASI GLASSWORKS

Riihimaen Lasi is situated about forty miles north of Helsinki. This glass factory, one of the largest and most diversified in Scandinavia, produces household glassware, containers, sheets, construction glass, and art glass.

The beginning of the Finnish glass industry goes back to the seventeenth century, but it was in 1910 that the production of hollow glass was started in Riihimaki. The 1920s, however, marked the real burgeoning of Finnish glassmaking art and design. Riihimaen Lasi, which now employs more than 1,000 people, has continued to benefit from the efforts of its group of dynamic designers. In fact, the history of the company has been marked by continuous expansion and rising production.

Founded partly in pursuit of the goal of Finnish nationalism, Riihimaen Lasi was the brainchild of three men: M. A. Kolehmainen, A. P. Kolehmainen, and H. G. Paloheimo. To start with, the works produced household glass, but soon began to cut crystal. From the beginning, there was an enthusiastic demand for its products, which are designed with both individuality and practical value in mind. Its glasses have a clear-cut and sophisticated but simple form that reveals the designers' awareness of and affection for the old Finnish crafts.

Although the factory has been making glass for six decades, it is constantly updating its products and plans to keep up with the spirit and demands of the present day. The creative power of its artists, together with the remarkable craftsmanship of Finnish glassblowers, has enabled the firm to make a significant contribution to the glassmaking and glass-designing tradition of Finland.

NANNY STILL

Elegance, grandeur, and generosity are often the hallmarks of Nanny Still's ornamental articles. Innovation is vital for her as an artist. In addition to her decorative glass, she has made a name for herself with exquisite wooden articles, including cutlery. Her "Flindari" glass series won her the American Institute of Interior Designers' Prize in 1965. She is truly one of the leading artists at Riihimaen Lasi. (See Color Plate 81.)

188.
Nanny Still, Finland. 10½".
Signed "Riihimaen Lasi oy, Finland, Nanny Still, Pompadour"

189.
Helena Tynell, Finland. 5″. Signed "H. Tynell
—Mushroom, Riihimaen Lasi oy, Finland"

HELENA TYNELL

Helena Tynell, well known for her highly individual designs, received the award of the American Institute of Interior Designers in 1968. She calls her decorative bottles "sun." All her pieces are single items, completely new forms, in that she lets hot liquid glass flow in various layers in iron molds. Because of the temperature difference, the material cools at different rates and therefore irregular folds and patterns are created. For all the designs she developed for Riihimaen Lasi Oy, Helena Tynell made drawings and prototypes out of wood, in order to demonstrate her ideas to the mold manufacturers and blowers in a plastic form, and to be able to discuss the various possibilities with the aid of the models. (See Color Plate 82.)

WARTSILA NOTSJO GLASSWORKS

This glassworks, now the oldest in Finland, was established in 1793. The Wartsila concern took over the works in 1950 as a complement to the Arabia porcelain factory. About 300 people are presently employed, doing manual blowing and pressing as well as automatic pressing.

Unique art glass augments the main assortment of high-quality household glass. Kaj Franck has designed glass for Notsjo since 1950; Oiva Toikka, 1963; and Heikki Orvola, 1969.

KAJ FRANCK

Born in Viipuri, Finland, November 9, 1911

This most professional of artists, while doing work that is quite simple and objective in design, is at the same time usually subtle in approach to his subject, occasionally displaying considerable humor. Recognition of his abilities has placed him in the position of art director of Oy Wartsila, Notsjoe Glass, where he has been employed at various times in his career. He attended the Institute of Industrial Arts, Department of Interior Decoration, and from 1960 to 1967 was art director at the Institute. His glass associations have always been with the top Finnish glasshouses. (See Color Plate 85.)

Prizes can usually be regarded as a neutral appraisal of an artist's work. Those Kaj Franck has received have been notable: the Lunning Prize, 1955; Diplome d'honneur, X Triennale, Milan, 1954; Gran Proemi, XI Triennale, Milan, 1957; Compasso d'Oro, 1957; and the prize of "Stockholms Tidningen," 1962. Among his exhibitions are:

"Design in Scandinavia," U.S.A. and Canada, 1954–57

"H–55," Halsingborg, Sweden, 1955

Milan Triennales: IX/1951, X/1954, XI/1957, XII/1960

"Tre Finska formgivare," Gothenburg and Copenhagen

Touring art exhibition, Germany 1956–57

Touring art exhibition, Rio de Janeiro, São Paulo, Buenos Aires, and Montevideo, 1958–59

190.
Kaj Franck, Finland. 13″. Signed "Kaj Franck, Notsjo"

Franck's works are in the following museums:

Kunstindustrimuseet, Copenhagen
Museum of Modern Art, New York
Nordfjeldske Kunstindustrimuseet, Trondheim, Norway
Rohnska Museet, Gothenburg, Sweden
Stedelijk Museum, Amsterdam, The Netherlands
Victoria and Albert Museum, London

◀191.
Kaj Franck, Finland. 9″. Signed "Kaj Franck, Nuutajarvi Notsjo"

192.▶
Kaj Franck, Finland. 5″. Signed "Kaj Franck, Nuutajarvi Notsjo"

193.
Kaj Franck, Finland. 13½″. Signed "Kaj Franck—Nuutajarvi Notsjo"

HEIKKI ORVOLA

Born in Helsinki, November 11, 1943

Hcikki Orvola attended the Institute of Industrial Arts, Department of Ceramics, from 1963 to 1968, after which—in 1970—he became an assistant instructor in that department. He has been employed by Oy Wartsila Ab, Notsjo Glass, since 1968. Orvola's work can be seen in the Museo Internazionale delle ceramiche, Faenza, Italy, and the Museum of Modern Art in New York City. (See Color Plate 89.)

194.	195.	196.
Heikki Orvola, Finland. 5″. Signed "Heikki Orvola, Nuutajarvi Notsjo"	Heikki Orvola, Finland. 7″. Signed "Heikki Orvola, Nuutajarvi Notsjo"	Heikki Orvola, Finland. 5½″. Signed "Heikki Orvola, Nuutajarvi Notsjo"

OIVA TOIKKA

Born in Viipuri, Finland, May 29, 1931

197. Oiva Toikka, Finland. 4″. Signed
"Oiva Toikka, Nuutajarvi Notsjo"

This important designer of excellent household glassware and decorative glass sculptures received his education at the Institute of Industrial Arts, Department of Ceramics, 1953–56, and the Art Teachers' Department, 1959–60. During this same period, he worked at Oy Wartsila Ab, Arabia, in the Art Department (1956–59), and taught general arts as well. In 1963 he joined the Notsjo glass division, where he has enjoyed an uninterrupted stay up to the present time. (See Color Plates 83 and 84.)

Oiva Toikka has been the recipient of several prizes and scholarships: Diploma 1969, "Internationales Kunsthandwerk," Stuttgart; the Lunning Prize, 1970; and the scholarship of the State of Finland, 1970.

His work may be seen in numerous museums, including The National Museum, Stockholm; Museum of Modern Art, New York; and the Victoria and Albert Museum, London.

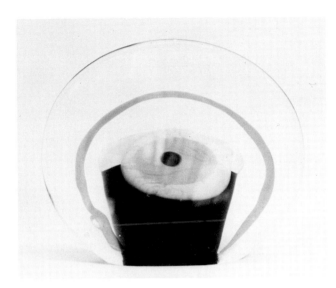

198. Oiva Toikka, Finland. 8¼". Signed "Oiva Toikka, Nuutajarvi Notsjo"

199. Oiva Toikka, Finland. 8½". Signed "Oiva Toikka, Nuutajarvi Notsjo"

◄200.
Oiva Toikka, Finland. 4½". Signed "Oiva Toikka, Nuutajarvi Notsjo"

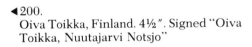

202.►
Oiva Toikka, Finland. 14". Signed "Oiva Toikka, Nuutajarvi Notsjo"

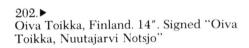

201.►
Oiva Toikka, Finland. 6¼". Signed "Oiva Toikka, Nuutajarvi Notsjo"

FRANCE

DAUM CRISTALLERIE DE NANCY

Many generations of master glassmakers have made the name Daum a synonym for good taste and quality, expressing first in glass and then in fine crystal the art and refinement of their time.

It was in 1875 that Jean Daum, together with a few glassmakers of the Lorraine and Franc-Contoise traditions, first opened an atelier, or workshop, in Nancy, France. In 1900 Antonin Daum, in his turn, achieved a triumph for his decorated glass at the Paris International Exhibition, and by then the School of Nancy had become recognized throughout the world. Again, at the International Exhibition of Decorative Arts in 1925, Paul Daum showed a new style of art in glass.

By 1950, like so many other glass companies, Henri and Michel Daum were concentrating on crystal, which was done in incomparable style by this great factory;

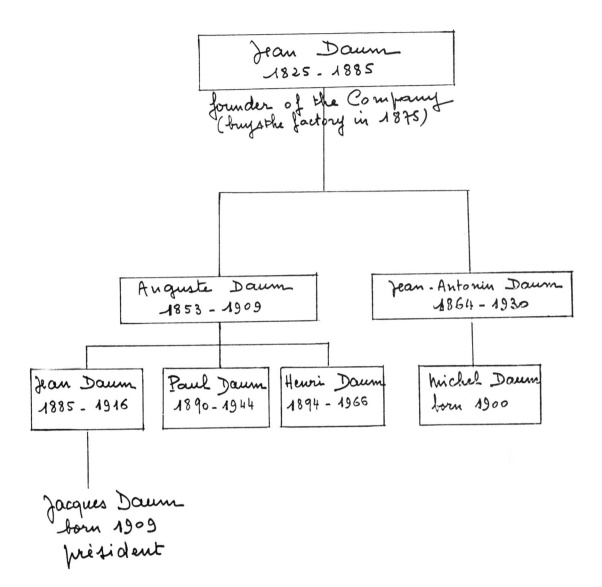

Jean Daum
1825 - 1885
founder of the Company
(buys the factory in 1875)

Auguste Daum
1853 - 1909

Jean - Antonin Daum
1864 - 1930

Jean Daum
1885 - 1916

Paul Daum
1890 - 1944

Henri Daum
1894 - 1966

Michel Daum
born 1900

Jacques Daum
born 1909
président

today it ranks with the best. Now under the leadership of Jacques Daum, the company is not restricting itself merely to a creditable routine production, but is blossoming out with an adventurous style of art. In 1968—with fantastic success—they began reproducing artworks by contemporary sculptors through the use of the pate de verre process. In this process, regular hard and finished colored glass is ground into a fine powder and mixed with a liquid, usually plain water, then heated in a mold. Normally, sectional molds are used, so there are duplicate pieces. Among the artists whose designs have been reproduced in glass by this technique are Salvador Dali, Paolo Santini, Maurice Legendre, Jean-Pièrre Demarchi, and Jacqueline Badord.

The family Daum can be justly proud of its magnificent heritage and creative future.

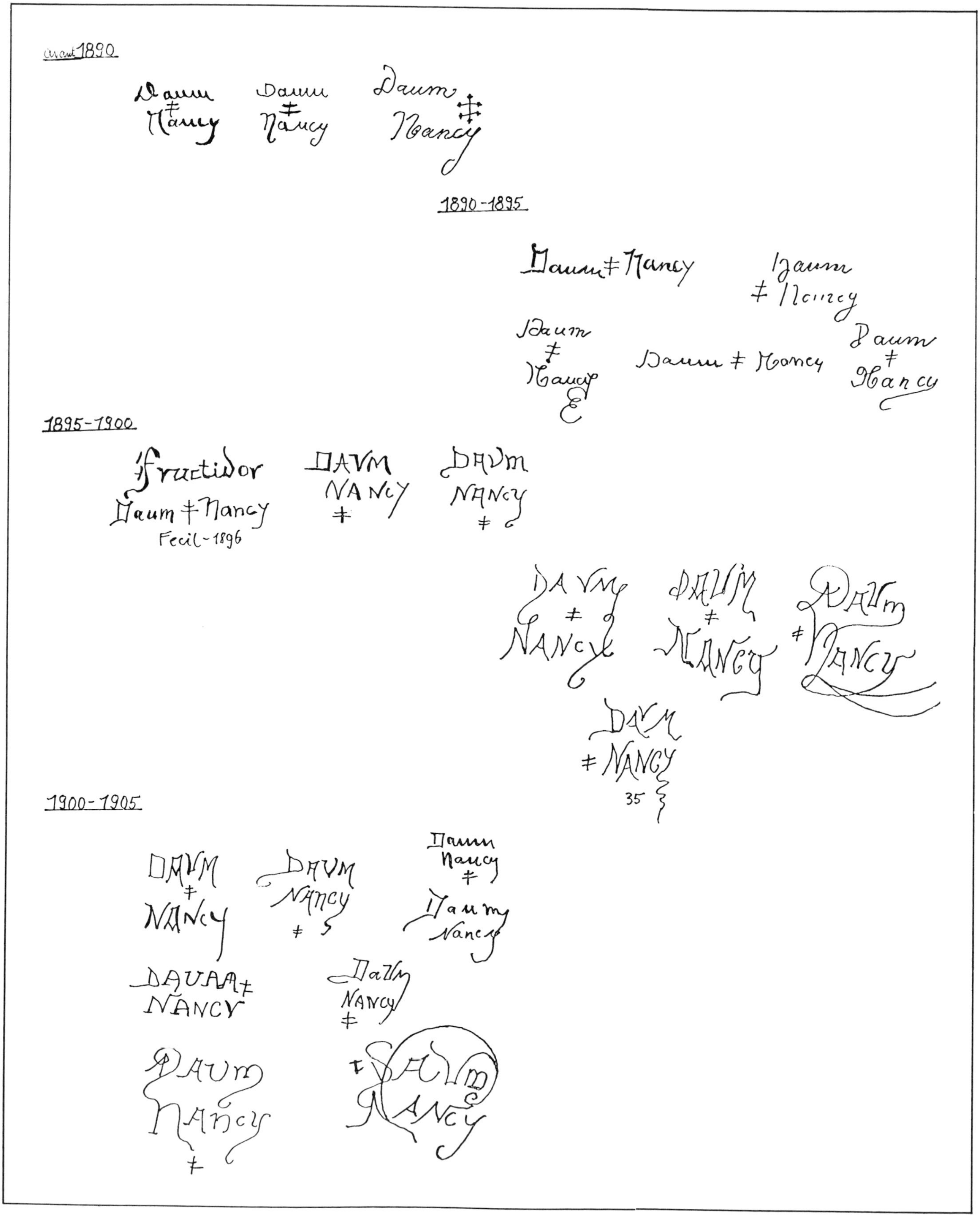

avant 1890

Daum
Nancy

Daum
Nancy

Daum
Nancy

1890-1895

Daum ✝ Nancy

Daum
✝ Nancy

Daum
✝
Nancy
E

Daum ✝ Nancy

Daum
✝
Nancy

1895-1900

Fructidor
Daum ✝ Nancy
Fecit-1896

DAVM
NANCY
✝

DAVM
NANCY
✝

DAVM
✝
NANCY

DAVM
✝
NANCY

DAVM
✝ NANCY

DAVM
✝ NANCY
35

1900-1905

DAVM
✝
NANCY

DAVM
NANCY
✝

Daum
Nancy
✝

Daum
Nancy

DAVAM✝
NANCY

Daum
Nancy
✝

DAVM
NANCY
✝

✝ DAVM
NANCY

1905-1910

DAUM ≠ Nancy

DAUM ≠ NANCY

DAUM NANCY ≠

Daum ≠ Nancy

DAUM NANCY

DAUM NANCY ≠

≠ DAUM et NANCY

1910-1915

DAUM Nancy ≠

DAUM NANCY ≠

Daum ≠ Nancy

DAUM ≠ NANCY FRANCE

DAUM ≠ NANCY

Vers 1920

57-E

DAUM ≠ Nancy

DAUM ≠ NANCY

DAUM Nancy ≠

DAUM ≠ NANCY FRANCE

Daum ≠ Nancy France

1947-1960   Daum ≠ France et Daum≠Nancy-France

1960 – 1971   Daum

JACQUELINE BADORD

Born in France, 1917

This recognized artist endeavors to create structures with a so called "poetic sensuality" and—in her own words—she tries "to attain this poetry by the sensuality of volumes, or of their interplay in space." (See Color Plate 88.) She has done many pieces for community projects, and has had a number of one-man exhibitions in Paris as well as at Aix-en-Provence, Amiens, and the Cultural Centre in both Tananarive and Réunion Island. She has also participated in shows in the Rodin Museum, Le Havre Museum, and the Musée d'Art Moderne.

SALVADOR DALI

Born in Figueras, Spain, 1904

There is no need to review the accomplishments of this internationally recognized figure in the world of art, nor the wide acceptance of his unique position by critics and experts. After a checkered career at the Fine Arts School in Madrid, in 1928 Dali met Picasso and the school of surrealist painters in Paris. He joined this movement in 1929, and did not part company with the group until 1939.

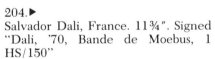

203.
Salvador Dali, France. 19½″. Signed "Daum, 1HS–150, Dali, 1970, Salvador Dali"

204.▶
Salvador Dali, France. 11¾″. Signed "Dali, '70, Bande de Moebus, 1 HS/150"

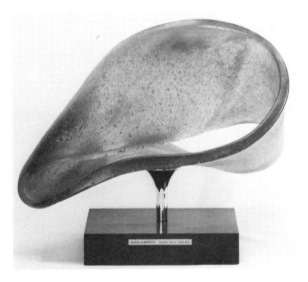

    Certainly Jacques Daum, in his position as director of the firm Daum et Cie, could have made no better choice than Dali of an original topflight artist to design suitable works for production as Daum pate de verre glass sculptures.

    Salvador Dali lives in Port Lligat, Cadaques, Spain. The translation of his work into the medium of glass has merely added a further dimension to his reputation. (See Color Plates 86 and 87.)

JEAN-PIERRE DEMARCHI

Born in France, 1928

A search for monumental art is characteristic of Demarchi's work in the world of imaginary sculptures. A student of Robert Couturier, he attended the Ecole Nationale Supérieure des Arts Décoratifs in Paris; he is now a member of the Société des Artistes Décorateurs de France.

Demarchi received the Fénéon Prize in 1960, and as the sculptor at the Paris Mint was the winner in the show "20 Years of Medals." He also received prizes at the Brussels International Exhibition in 1958 and the Paris Triennale in 1959. He is responsible for the Monument to the Résistance in Vigneux-sur-Seine, and has participated in a variety of exhibitions in Paris and in Oslo, Rome, and Helsinki. (See Color Plate 91.)

MAURICE LEGENDRE

Born in Paris, 1928

Maurice Legendre has expressed his viewpoint very succinctly: "Every technique presents a new problem . . . in particular, glass paste that provides translucency. It is with humility that, basing myself on this material, I attempt to show the tragic and laughable aspect of a vanishing world." It might be said the Legendre treats animal themes, human forms, and monumental art with considerable passion and violence, but this is not an unusual approach in creating sculptures of any material. (See Color Plate 90.)

Formerly a student at the Ecole Nationale Supérieure des Arts Décoratifs and a pupil of Robert Couturier and Marcel Gimond, Legendre is now a member of the Société des Artistes Décorateurs de France. In 1954 he won the Blumenthal Prize. In addition to being shown at many international museums, his works have been acquired by the French Government and the Musée d'Art Moderne in Paris. Currently Legendre makes his home in Paris.

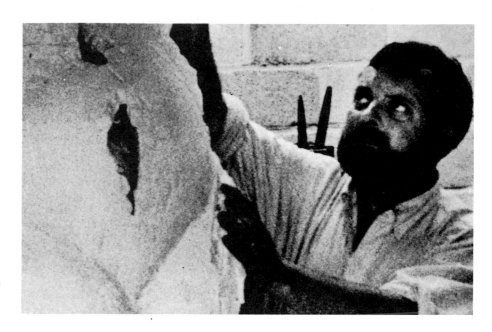

M.Legendre

PAOLO SANTINI

Born in Florence, Italy, 1929

Santini

Paolo Santini studied at the Turin School of Fine Arts. Although living in Paris, he attributes his tireless imagination and baroque approach to sculpture to remaining "isolated, out of the world, in communication with the earth." Santini has contributed to the success of many Paris exhibitions. (See Color Plate 93.)

ISRAEL

205. Ariel Bar-Tal, Israel. 16″. Signed "Bar-Tal"

ARIEL BAR-TAL

Bar-Tal, born in Budapest in 1920, started to learn drawing and painting there as a schoolboy. However, prevented by the prewar regime in Hungary from completing his studies at the Academy of Fine Arts, he turned to blowing glass scientific apparatus as a practical occupation. After spending the war years in concentration camps, Bar-Tal went to Rome, where he completed his training, studying sculpture and the history of arts and crafts and at the same time working as a blower of scientific glass.

Sculpture in glass, as understood by the artist, is different from the ancient casting of statuettes in molds or from carving glass as if it were stone. Here the shapes are obtained through blowing and repeated heating, a process that common glass cannot stand. The borosilicate glass known as Pyrex, first used for scientific apparatus, provided the artist with a material of the required plastic qualities. It can be cooled and reheated as many times as is necessary because of its very low coefficient of expansion. But since Pyrex is available only as a transparent colorless glass, there arose the technical-aesthetic problem of coloring it. Moreover, this glass does not take enameling. Bar-Tal devoted years of work and research to developing a staining technique. This consists of evaporating metal salts in the flame during the forming process, thus creating a colored skin on the surface that cannot be removed.

There is no essential difference between Bar-Tal's sculptures and his vessels, which are sculptured forms too, derived frequently from plastic experiments and adapted just enough to function as a vase, urn, or jar. He likes to give them a textured surface somewhat resembling the patina of ancient glass, but his emphasis is always on the sculptural form, leaving to color and texture a secondary role. To quote from an essay he wrote about contemporary glass: "The ultimate justification in aesthetic terms of any artistic vessel of glass or of any other material, whether it is pottery, wood, or silver, is determined by its plastic form."

The first exhibition of the work of Ariel Bar-Tal, held in Tel Aviv in 1960, was brought to the attention of Baroness Bethsabee de Rothschild, who commissioned him to create artistic objects for the Bat-Sheva Crafts Corporation in Tel Aviv. Baroness de Rothschild has continued to take a close personal interest in the career of this artist and since then has been his mentor.

In 1961 he was invited to show his work at Tiffany's in New York. Success was so great that another exhibition followed in 1962 at the same place. In 1967 he had a one-man show at the Haaretz Museum in Tel Aviv. In her book *Glass and Crystal*, the Dutch art critic Elka Schrijver comments as follows:

> Bar-Tal was greatly impressed by the exquisite beauty of the ancient glass in the Haaretz Museum, and encouraged both by the museum's director and the Crafts Centre already mentioned. He too allowed himself to be inspired by the classic shapes and sheens, though in a vastly superior manner. Bar-Tal is a great artist. The work he showed at Tiffany's in New York a few years ago has rightly been hailed as among the most beautiful glass in our time.

During his visit to Paris in 1962, Bar-Tal came upon a new and successful art called "gemmaux," which had been developed by a group of Frenchmen. *Gemmaux* are pictures made entirely of glass, by sticking on and superimposing, in a sort of three-dimensional mosaic, tiny pieces of colored glass. Exploiting the light-breaking quality of glass, the makers of *gemmaux* create an almost kinetic effect. Artists like Braque, Picasso, Rouault, Matisse, and Cocteau were among the enthusiasts and practitioners of this new art.

Captivated by the crystalline vibrations of *gemmaux*, Bar-Tal tried for and succeeded in obtaining almost the same effect by fusing the tiny pieces of glass is a flat organic unit. After four years of experiments, he produced a technique that in some ways is the reverse of the *gemmaux* technique. He paints on glass sheet with colorant oxides. Once the picture is finished, it is fused in a kiln into a flat, united piece. After cooling, under the influence of certain chemicals millions of tiny crackings are produced, which transform the glass sheet into a conglomerate of tiny glass crystals.

Bar-Tal is one of the few glass artists able both to conceive and to realize his own work. His artistic talent and thorough knowledge of the secrets of glassmaking have combined to give a characteristic spontaneity to his work. (See Color Plate 92.)

ITALY

Alfredo Barbini [signature]

ALFREDO BARBINI and the BARBINI GLASSWORKS

In the first years of the seventeenth century, decrees issued by Podesta Coriolano Benzon and Podesta Gabriello Barbarigo, with the approval of Prince Marino Grimani, opened the Gold Book of Murano Island for the listing of all persons entitled to Murano citizenship. Among those listed were four members of the family Barbini: Ser Francesco, Ser Steffano, Ser Iseppo, and Ser Zorzi. Among the privileges granted those whose names were inscribed in the Gold Book was the right to hunt game and to sit on the Murano Island Council. They were also permitted to manufacture and to work glass.

The family Barbini exercised this last privilege with consummate skill, though some Barbinis branched out in other areas of artistic endeavor. One, Michelangelo Barbini, was a fine portrait artist, and was presented at Napoleon's Court in 1805.

Alfredo Barbini is a descendant of those early-day glass manufacturers and workers. His is a heritage of artistry. He has been showered with critical acclaim as a singularly fine innovator in glass design. It seems inevitable, in view of his ancestry, that Barbini should have turned to glass for a career. His father's family was interested primarily in the manufacture of glass beads, but from his maternal ancestors he derived an interest in artistic hand-blown and engraved glass.

As a boy, Alfredo Barbini often wandered through the famous glass museum not too far from his island home. The museum's walls are hung with portraits of famous persons of Muranese origin. One of Barbini's ancestors, Dr. Vincenzo Barbini, is represented in a portrait in the main hall of the museum. Thus inspired, young Alfredo was determined to achieve fame as an artist in glass—although his parents were determined to guide him into other areas of endeavor, he nonetheless persisted in answering the call of the furnace.

At ten, Alfredo attended Abate Zanetti, a design school attached to the Murano glass museum. There he learned the art of decorating glass with enamel, and took his first faltering steps toward a comprehension of colors. Thereafter, he was apprenticed to the Ferro-Toso glass factory. In 1930, at the age of nineteen, he entered the Cristalleria de Murano, where fine work was being done in the production of artistic glass. He achieved the title of Maestro at the Cristalleria, and became adept in the manipulation of glass and the achievement of colorful designs.

206.
Alfredo Barbini, Italy. 6". Signed "Alfredo Barbini, Murano, 1970"

207.▶
Alfredo Barbini, Italy. 10½". Signed "Alfredo Barbini, Murano, 1970"

208.
Alfredo Barbini, Italy. 4¼". Signed "Alfredo Barbini"

There was a stay in Milan later, followed by a term of service as Primo Maestro at the glass factory of Zecchin & Martinuzzi, directed by Napoleone Martinuzzi, a sculptor of prominence. Working with Martinuzzi, Barbini was able to achieve designs beyond even his fondest dreams in the sculpture of glass. Just before the war, he became a partner in a firm called Vamsa, and worked hard at developing new techniques of engraving glass. Next, he pursued even more advanced methods of sculpture on glass and, in the course of this effort, specialized in knickknacks made of block glass. The block technique was new to Murano glassworkers; it replaced the former use of spun glass, which did not provide either skeleton or plastic consistency.

Finally, in 1948 and 1950, at the biennial exhibitions in Venice, Barbini put his unique pieces on display. They were immediately endorsed by the critics because of their originality and coloration. (See Color Plates 95, 97, and 101.) Inspired by this acclaim, Barbini has been working at his own furnace ever since 1950 and has exhibited in the United States, Chile, France, Sweden, Germany, Denmark, England, and Ireland. In 1955, the Italian government gave him the Croce de Cavaliere al Merito—recognizing him as an artist.

 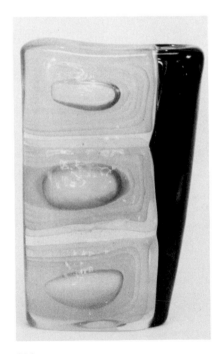 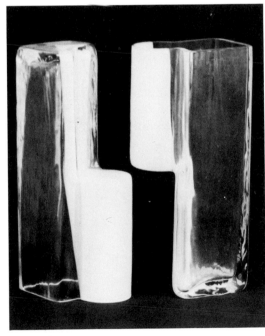

209.
Alfredo Barbini, Italy. 8″. Signed "Alfredo Barbini, Murano, 1970"

210.
Alfredo Barbini, Italy. 10½″. Signed "Alfredo Barbini, Murano, 1970"

211.
Alfredo Barbini, Italy. 10″. Signed "Alfredo Barbini, Murano, 1970"

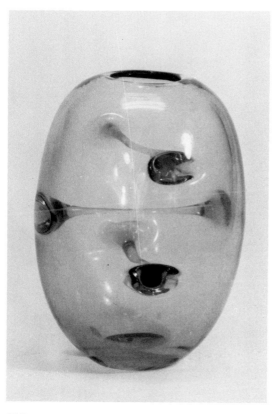

212.
Alfredo Barbini, Italy. 12″. Signed "Alfredo Barbini, Murano, 1970"

213.
Alfredo Barbini, Italy. 10″. Signed "Alfredo Barbini, Murano, 1970"

214.
Alfredo Barbini, Italy. 3″. Signed "Alfredo Barbini, Murano, 1970"

215.▶
Alfredo Barbini, Italy. 13″. Signed "Alfredo Barbini, Murano, 1970"

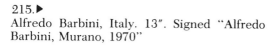

Ercole Barovier

Angelo Barovier 1971

BAROVIER AND TOSO

The art of glassmaking flourished on Murano throughout the Italian Renaissance, in the fifteenth and sixteenth centuries. During this period one particular glass family rose to preeminence: the Baroviers. They pushed the art of blowing glass to levels of versatility, expressiveness, and elegance unknown before.

An early member of this family, Angelo Barovier, discovered and developed new techniques for coloring glassware and painting on glass. He was greatly praised by the Venetians as the foremost artist of his age, and received many honors and rewards. A few of his works are still extant, such as the famous wedding cup (about 1437) now in the glass museum in Murano. From his sons, Davide, Pietro, and Giovanni, the family divided into three branches, all of which produced leading glass artists in the following centuries. During this period other great glass families, including the Ballarin and the Dalla Luna, also were active at Murano.

Ercole Barovier inherited the firm Artisti Barovier from his father after the

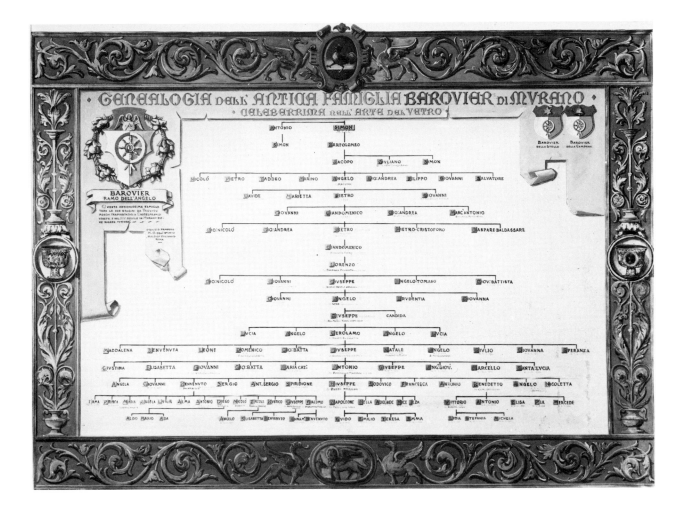

First World War. In 1936 he founded a new factory, Barovier and Toso, with the brothers Artemio and Decio Toso, whose family traced their glass traditions back to the seventeenth century. Their unique designs soon won increasing artistic and commercial success. Both an artist and chemist, Ercole is—after forty years—still the chief designer of this firm.

During his career, Ercole Barovier has created and exhibited more than 25,-000 different models of vases, bowls, chandeliers, figurines, and other decorative accessories, as well as discovered new technical processes and developed new compounds for coloring. Since he first showed his work in 1925 he has been represented at all the most important art exhibitions—the Biennales in Venice, the Triennales in Milan, the universal exhibitions in Brussels, New York, Paris, Berlin, and Montreal. His pieces are also in the collections of the Victoria and Albert Museum and the South Kensington Museum in London, the Louvre in Paris, the Corning Museum of Glass in the United States, the Curtius Museum in Liège, the National Glassmuseum of Leerdam in The Netherlands, and in others.

The Barovier and Toso Furance, now one of the leading firms in Murano, is headed by Ercole Barovier as president and art manager; technical and commercial managers are still, respectively, Decio and Artemio Toso. Representing the younger generation is Ercole's son, Angelo, a widely exhibited painter and glass designer, who is export manager. Decio's son, Piero Toso, manages the architectural lighting office.

The glass of this firm is unmistakably individualistic and artistic. (See Color Plate 100 [A. Barovier], 102 [E. Barovier], and 104 [Toso].)

216.
Ercole Barovier, Italy. 10″. Signed "Ercole Barovier"

217.
Ercole Barovier, Italy. 9½″. Signed "Ercole Barovier, 1970"

218.
Ercole Barovier, Italy. 5½″. Signed "Ercole Barovier, 1970"

219.
Ercole Barovier, Italy. 8¼″. Signed "Ercole Barovier, 1970"

SALVIATI & COMPANY

The first in the long chain of Salviati glassmen was Antonio Salviati, Commander of the Crown of Italy, who in 1856 established a glass manufactory. He became the friend and leader of a group of the best artists in the Murano of his day. The restoration of the town's classical blown-glass industry began with the works of the Salviati factory, and continued with the founding of many other factories devoted exclusively to the making of the finest Venetian glass.

In 1896 the establishments of Salviati were directed by Maurice Camerino; starting as manager, he became the sole proprietor. Because of his energy, his great love for the noble art of glassmaking, and long years of indefatigable work, he gave new direction to the Salviati enterprise.

In the 1920s Maurice Camerino's sons, Mario and Renzo, began active work in the firm. Renzo is now president, and a grandson of Maurice Camerino, Renzo Tedeschi, is working with him as chairman of the board of directors. These new generations have enhanced the tradition and prestige of the Salviati name by availing themselves of the services of designers and architects who have adapted the characteristics of the old Venetian glassblowing art to modern taste and to the needs of modern living. Among the important designers of Salviati glass are Luciano Gaspari, Alberto Rosselli, Sergio Asti, Bertha and Teff Sarasin, Ward Bennett, Franco Albini, and Franca Helg. (See Color Plate 99.)

Renzo Camerino, born on April 13, 1904, has been most successful in all phases of glass activity. He was the instigator of the first Italian Industries Design School; he has also been president of the Venice Art Institute, which was enlarged and renovated under his aegis. Recently he was awarded the honor Cavaliere del Lavoro, and in addition "The Golden Compass" was assigned to the enterprise he directs (Salviati & C.) as a reward for the fruitful activity it has conducted over so many years. He has not only realized the importance of the commercial aspects of his field but also recognized the importance to his company of the many creative, artistic, and cultural developments in the world today, as all the leading factories do.

Permanent exhibitions of Salviati glass are in the following:

Corning Museum of Glass, Corning, New York

Kestner Museum, Hanover, West Germany

Musée du Verre, Liège, Belgium

Museum Haaretz, Tel Aviv, Israel

Museum of Modern Art, New York

Victoria and Albert Museum, London

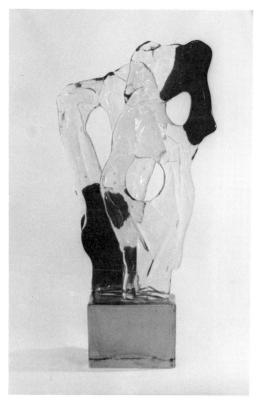

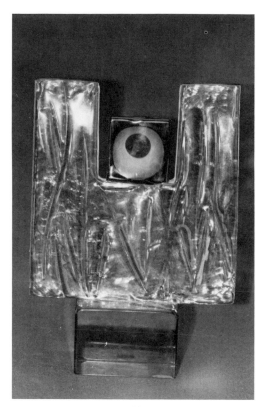

220.
Salviati & Co., Italy. 19½″. Signed "Salviati & Co."

221.
Salviati & Co., Italy. 12¼″. Signed "Salviati & Co."

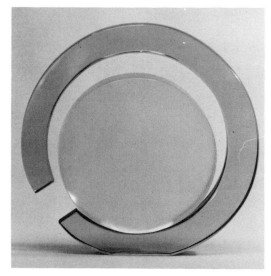

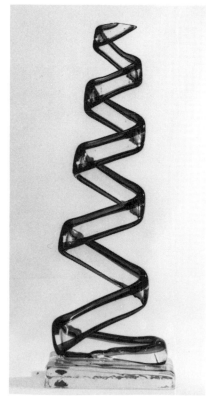

222.
Salviati & Co., Italy. 11″. Signed "Salviati & Co."

223.
Salviati & Co., Italy. 19½″. Signed "Salviati & Co."

VENINI GLASSWORKS

Paolo Venini established his glass factory in Murano in 1925. He was born in 1895 into a family with connections in the glass industry, and at first he worked as a pure experimentalist, reviving old Venetian color techniques and inventing new ones. Venini was also a perfectionist who was, to a large extent, his own designer. His wonderful skill, great taste, and the superior quality of his glass were the rare combination that made the Venini Glass Company outstanding throughout the world.

Today his daughter and son-in-law, Mr. and Mrs. Ludovico Diaz De Santillana, carry on his work and invite free-lance designers to Murano. The artistic creativity of men such as Tapio Wirkkala, who designed the recent pieces for Venini, inspires glassmakers everywhere. Wirkkala has won gold and silver medals at the Triennale —seven Grand Prix in Milan alone, among countless other awards.

In addition to directing the operations of the firm, Ludovico Diaz De Santillana takes a personal hand in designing individual pieces. (See Color Plate 106.)

TAPIO WIRKKALA

The versatile artistic talent of Tapio Wirkkala is such that it defies definition. For instance, as mentioned, he has won seven Grand Prix and one gold medal at the Milan Triennales, and has won in five different branches of art: light fittings, art glass, sculpture, wood, and exhibition planning. He has also produced beautiful creations in silver and porcelain. The broad range of interests of this artist and his high standards have brought him innumerable other prizes, such as a prize in 1947 for new bank notes in a competition held by the Bank of Finland. In 1951 he won the Lunning Prize, as the best designer in Scandinavia. The year 1952 brought him four awards in a competition for Olympic Games stamps. For a sterling silver flatware design, he was recognized by the Museum of Contemporary Crafts in 1960. Wirkkala received awards in the Faenza International Ceramic Competition in 1963, 1966, 1967, and 1969; in 1963 he also received the Golden Obelisk in Milan. An honorary degree was conferred on him by the Royal College of Art in 1971.

Today, with the liveliness of international communication and the virtual absence of design copyrights, design ideas are soon adopted almost universally. In Wirkkala's estimation, this poses a problem for the designer: Should he stick to his own inspiration or be swayed by foreign trends? Confronted with this situation, a designer must have a true creative ability upon which he can depend. "I myself flee mannerism by changing over to another type of design once it begins to feel like 'work,' " says this artist. "It requires immense effort and a new start every time, but only in this way can something new be created." (See Color Plate 103.)

Wirkkala graduated from the Industrial Art Institute, Helsinki, in 1936. He was art director of Taideteollinen Oppilaito, Helsinki, from 1951 to 1954, and in 1955 collaborated with Raymond Loewy Associates in New York. Over the years, he has been associated with a number of firms; at present he is working with Venini, where he has achieved his most fluent expression in art glass. Wirkkala is represented in the permanent collections of the following major museums:

Kunstgewerbemuseum, Zurich, Switzerland

Metropolitan Museum of Art, New York

Museum of Modern Art, New York

National Museum, Stockholm

Nordfjeldske Kunstindustriemuseet, Trondheim, Norway

University Museum, Mexico City

Victoria and Albert Museum, London

His work has been shown widely in exhibitions throughout Europe as well as in a Smithsonian Institution traveling show, at the Montreal World's Fair in 1967, and the Mexico Culture Olympics in 1968. Tapio and his wife Rut Bryk had a two-man show in the United States from 1956 to 1958. Wirkkala has, as well, served as the "architect" of a number of strictly Finnish exhibitions that have appeared in other lands—Sweden, Switzerland, England, Austria, France, The Netherlands, Denmark, Hungary, Belgium, West Germany, and the U.S.S.R.

224.
Tapio Wirkkala, Italy. 8¼″. Signed
"Venini, Italia, 1969, Tapio Wirkkala"

225.
Tapio Wirkkala, Italy. 12″. Signed
"Venini, Italia, 1970, Tapio Wirkkala.

226.
Tapio Wirkkala, Italy. 15½″. Signed
"Venini, Italia, 1969, Tapio Wirkkala"

GIANCARLO BEGOTTI

See Color Plate 107.

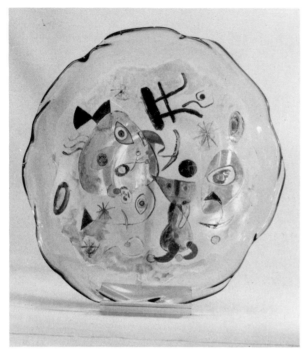

227. Giancarlo Begotti, Italy. 16¾″. Signed "G. Begotti, '58"

228. Giancarlo Begotti, Italy. 17¾″. Signed "Giancarlo Begotti, 1965"

229. Giancarlo Begotti, Italy. 14½″. Signed "G. Begotti"

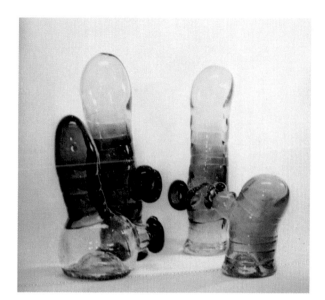

Plate 70.   Per Lutken, Denmark. 9½ inches. Signed "1970 Per Lutken Holmegaard #396"

Plate 71.   John H. Cook, England. Taller piece, 10½ inches.

Plate 72.   John H. Cook, England. 8 inches. Signed "John H. Cook, 1970"

Plate 73.   Tockstein-Frohlich, Czechoslovakia. 5¾ inches. Signed "Tockstein-Frohlich/Circus"

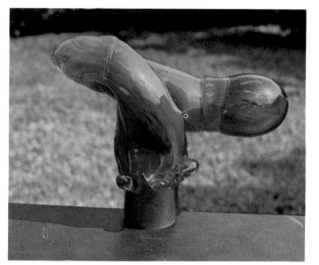

Plate 74. Dillon Clarke, England. Piece in center, 18¼ inches.

Plate 75. Keith Cummings, England. 6¾ inches. Signed "Keith Cummings, 1969"

Plate 76. Samuel J. Herman, England. 9 inches. Signed "Samuel J. Herman, 1970"

Plate 77. Samuel J. Herman, England. 9½ inches. Signed "Samuel J. Herman, 1971"

Plate 78.   Pauline Solven, England. 11½ and 16¾ inches.

Plate 79.   Samuel J. Herman, England. Piece in center, 7½ inches.

Plate 80.   Samuel J. Herman, England. 8¼ inches. Signed "Samuel J. Herman 1971"

Plate 81.   Nanny Still, Finland. 6 inches. Signed "Nanny Still, Riihimaen Lasi/Turmaline"

Plate 82. Helena Tynell, Finland. 8 inches. Signed "Helena Tynell, Riihimaen Lasi"

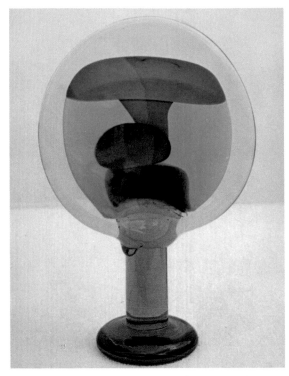

Plate 83. Oiva Toikka, Finland. 10¾ inches. Signed "Oiva Toikka, Nuutajarvi Notsjo"

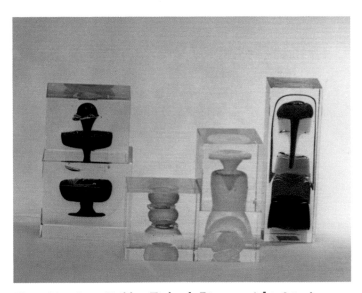

Plate 84. Oiva Toikka, Finland. Piece at **right**, 6 inches.

Plate 85. Kaj Franck, Finland. 12¼ inches. Signed "Kaj Franck, Nuutajarvi Notsjo"

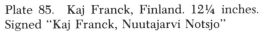

Plate 86. Salvador Dali, France. 13½ inches.
Signed "Dali 1967, HS/250, 'Pegasus' Daum"

Plate 87. Salvador Dali, France. 16 inches.
Signed "Daum–HS/150, Salvador Dali 1970,
'L'Anti Fleur' "

Plate 88. Jacqueline Badord, France (Daum).
17 inches.

Plate 89. Heikki Orvola, Finland. 6¼ and 3¾
inches.

Plate 90.   Maurice Legendre, France (Daum). 14¾
inches.

Plate 91.   Jean-Pierre Demarchi, France. 11½
inches.

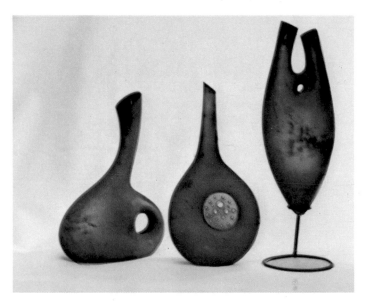

Plate 92.   Bar-Tal, Israel. Tallest piece, 13 inches.

Plate 93.   Paolo Santini, France. 16½ inches.
Signed "Santini 'Neutron' 1968–150, Daum"

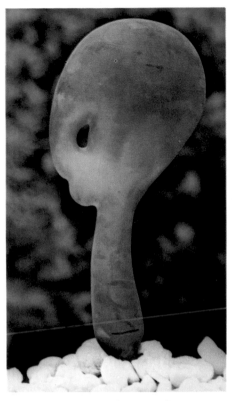

Plate 94. Bar-Tal, Israel. 15 inches. Signed "Bar Tal 1971"

Plate 95. Alfredo Barbini, Italy. 8½ inches. Signed "Alfredo Barbini Murano, 1970"

Plate 96. Sybren Valkema, The Netherlands. 11½ inches. Signed "Sybren Valkema, Leerdam, Unica, VV5LL"

Plate 97. Alfredo Barbini, Italy. 11 inches. Signed "Alfredo Barbini"

Plate 98. Sybren Valkema, The Netherlands. 9¾ inches. Signed "Sybren Valkema, Leerdam, Unica, VV4LL"

Plate 99. Salviati & Company, Italy. 10¾ inches.
Signed "Venice, Italy, Salviati & Co."

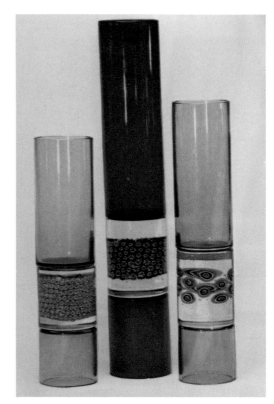

Plate 100. Angelo Barovier, Italy. Piece in
center, 19¾ inches.

Plate 102. Ercole Barovier, Italy. 11½ inches.
Signed "Ercole Barovier, 1970"

Plate 101. Alfredo Barbini, Italy. Piece in center, 5 inches.

230. Giancarlo Begotti, Italy. 15¼". Signed "Giancarlo Begotti, 1957"

231. Giancarlo Begotti, Italy. 17". Signed "Giancarlo Begotti, 1957"

THE NETHERLANDS

LEERDAM GLASSWORKS

In 1878 a new glass manufacturing company was founded in Leerdam in the Netherlands. For many years it made only bottles and cheap household ware, but in 1915 experimentation with new techniques and the hiring of fine artist-designers changed the quality of its output. In 1917 the man who was to make Leerdam world famous, Andries Dirk Copier, joined the company as a designer, when he was just sixteen years old.

Copier succeeded in cutting heavy glass in large facets to create uniquely beautiful works of glass art. It was he who began the famed Leerdam Glass School and attracted so many promising young artists there. Today Copier is artistic director of the firm, justly well known for his remarkable achievements.

Sybren Valkema, who has served as joint director of the Amsterdam School for the Applied Arts, is a designer at Leerdam too. His imaginative sculptural forms in glass have won wide recognition.

SYBREN VALKEMA

Born in The Hague, August 13, 1916
Wife (2nd): Veronica Valkema-Kindermans
Son (by first marriage): Wybe Valkema
Son (by second marriage): Dirk, a student
of glass and ceramics at Rietveld Academy

Production glass
1953 (never used)

Unique pieces ceramic
De Porceleyne Fles Delft
1956–1962

Sample:
V = Valkema
O = 1966
132 = from 1 until the end
of the year with diamond
scratched into the bottom

Undoubtedly one of the very important artists in the field of glass, Sybren Valkema has established a reputation as an outstanding international teacher and a leader among his associates. He is involved both with the World Craft Council and the Ministry of Culture in The Netherlands, and is one of the directors of Rietveld Academy, responsible for organizing the programs in all departments. He also is associated with a half dozen other influential professional groups.

Valkema graduated in 1936 as a primary school teacher; until 1940, he pursued graduate studies in art education at the Royal Academy of Art in The Hague. His first teaching was done at the Royal Academy and the Leerdam Glass School; then he taught at the School of Applied Arts in Amsterdam, where he became associate director from 1951 to 1971. In the course of his career, Valkema has worked with Erwin Eisch, Sam Herman, Harvey Littleton, and Marvin Lipofsky, exchanging ideas, methods of approach to the studio-glass field, and actually blowing glass in one another's studios.

As a visiting professor of art, in 1968 Valkema replaced Harvey Littleton, who was on leave from the University of Wisconsin, and conducted a special program dealing with European glass techniques. During that same year Valkema joined Littleton at the University of California, Berkeley, at the "Great Glass Symposium" organized by Marvin Lipofsky. In 1969, he himself organized a traveling exhibition in The Netherlands made up of the work of these glass pioneers.

After 1947, Valkema's work began to be featured in international as well as national group exhibitions, as is evident from the following partial chronological list:

Stedelijk Museum, Amsterdam, 1947

"Manifestation E 55," Rotterdam, 1955

Museum Boymans–van Beuningen, Rotterdam, 1955

Triennale, Milan, Italy, 1957

Osthaus Museum, Hagen, West Germany, 1957

Expo Bruxelles, Belgium, 1962

Traveling exhibition in the U.S.A., 1962–63

University of Wisconsin, 1968

Museum of Applied Arts, Prague, Czechoslovakia, 1970

Landesmuseum, Oldenburg, West Germany, 1971

Valkema's work is also represented in the following permanent collections:

Corning Museum of Glass, Corning, New York

Museum Boymans–van Beuningen, Rotterdam

National Glass Museum, Leerdam

Netherlands Embassy, Washington, D.C.

State Collection of The Netherlands

Stedelijk Museum, Amsterdam

University of Wisconsin, Madison, Wisconsin

Because of Valkema's vast knowledge and competence in the field of glass, his accomplishments have been the subject of numerous articles in magazines and trade publications. (See Color Plates 96 and 98.)

232.
Sybren Valkema, The Netherlands. 9¼". Signed "Sybren Valkema, Leerdam"

NORWAY

HADELAND GLASSWORKS

For over 200 years the Hadeland Glassworks of Jevnaker, Norway, has been in continuous production. The unique character and style of its glass is due in no small degree to the fact that Hadeland was among the first industrial concerns in Norway to employ people for their artistic talent—the forerunners of today's industrial designers. This policy has won for Hadeland and its staff many outstanding design and quality awards at exhibitions throughout Europe. Willy Johansson, for example, received the Diplome d'honneur, the gold medal and silver medal at the Milan Triennales in 1954 and 1960.

The factory was founded in 1762 for the express purpose of producing bottles for the domestic market. The site at Jevnaker was chosen with great care, the rich forests along the fjord ensuring a plentiful supply of fuel for years to come. In 1850, however, a radical change took place: the manufacture of household glass and of their peerless heavy lead crystal was initiated. This gradually superseded the bottlemaking, and now the name of Hadeland is synonymous with glass tableware and fine lead crystal. Today the glass tradition of this factory is carried on by designers and craftsmen whose creative skills are directed toward modern design allied with an appreciation of and respect for the meaning of true craftsmanship.

Many people have had an influence on the development of Hadeland, but it is the Berg family that is dominant. Since the 1850s they have led the concern, and today Jens W. Berg, a civil engineer, represents the sixth generation of the family to occupy the director's chair. He is well qualified for the task of running a modern yet traditional glassworks. After completing his academic studies, he traveled extensively to study the glass industries of other countries, and brought back valuable new plans and ideas to Hadeland.

233.
Jon Gundersen, Norway. 14¼".
Signed "Jon Gundersen, Norway, Hadeland, F.S."

SEVERIN BRORBY

Born in Norway, October 19, 1932

Severin Brorby was engaged by Hadeland Glassworks in 1948 to work in the engraving department; he still continues his association with the firm, now in the design department. (See Color Plate 108.)

Brorby trained at the State School of Applied Arts and Crafts in Oslo from 1952 through 1955. In 1966 and 1967 he was awarded the City of Oslo Scholarship known as "The Badge of Good Design." During 1966 he traveled and studied in Canada and the United States. Brorby's work is in the following museums:

> Corning Museum of Glass, Corning, New York
> Museum of Applied Arts, Oslo, Norway
> Nordfjeldske Kunstindustrimuseet, Trondheim, Norway
> Vestlandske Museum of Applied Arts, Bergen, Norway

He has also participated in the following exhibitions:

> "H–55," Halsingborg, Sweden, 1955
> School of Decorative Art (autumn show), 1957
> "Glass 1959," international show at Corning Museum of Glass
> Triennale (XII), Milan, Italy, 1960
> "Nordiska Formgivare," Gothenburg, Sweden, 1962

WILLY JOHANSSON

Born in Jevnaker, Norway, May 2, 1921

Johansson trained at the State School of Applied Arts and Crafts, Oslo, from 1939 to 1942, and in the 1945–47 period attended evening classes at the same school. He first worked in the Hadeland Glassworks in the sandblasting section under the leadership of Stale Kyllingstad (1942–45) and was later (1947) engaged as a full-time designer by Hadeland Glassworks, where he continues at the present time. (See Color Plate 105.)

Awarded honors at the X, XI, and XII (1954, 1957, and 1960) Triennales in Milan, Italy, he has received numerous scholarships as well: Decorative Art State Scholarship, 1957; Schaffergaard Scholarship, 1963; and Travel and Study State Scholarship for Artists, 1965. In 1966, he received the "Badge for Good Design." That same year he had a one-man exhibition at the Artists' Centre in Oslo, which afterward was shown in the museums in Trondheim, Bergen, and Drammen. In 1968, Johansson was nominated for the American Institute of Interior Designers. He is represented in the following museums:

Corning Museum of Glass, Corning, New York

Landeswerbes Museum, Baden-Wurttemberg, West Germany

Malmo Museum, Malmo, Sweden

Museum of Applied Arts, Oslo, Norway

Nordenfjeldske Kunstindustrimuseet, Trondheim, Norway

Oslo Foreign Office, Cultural Section, Permanent Collection

Rohnska Museum of Arts, Gothenburg, Sweden

Society of Decorative Art, Permanent Collection, Oslo

Vestlandske Museum of Applied Arts, Bergen, Norway

GRO SOMMERFELT

Born in Norway, October 30, 1940

After earning a diploma from the State School of Applied Arts and Crafts, Oslo, in 1960, Gro Sommerfelt spent three months studying at Dannegrog Weavers and Material Printers in Amsterdam. In 1961 she was engaged in the textile printing section of the Plus Centre, Fredrikstad, Norway, and in 1964 graduated from the Teachers State School of Drawing and Woodwork Education. Christiania Glasmagasin then employed her as designer. In 1968 she was awarded the Johan Helmich and Marcia Jansons Legacy. For the last few years Mrs. Sommerfelt has been associated with Hadeland Glassworks. (See Color Plate 110.)

234.
Gro Sommerfelt, Norway. 5". Signed "Hadeland, Norway, 1971, Gro Sommerfelt"

BENNY MOTZFELDT

Benny Motzfeldt was born in 1909 in central Norway north of Trondheim, where her father was a country doctor. She was graduated from college and had four years at the Arts and Crafts School in Oslo. She is married to Lt. Gen. (ret.) B. F. Motzfeldt, former chief of staff of the Royal Norwegian Air Force, and has one daughter, Eva, a Red Cross nurse. Aside from her glass work, Mrs. Motzfeldt's main interests are botany and painting.

Benny Motzfeldt started working in glass by answering an advertisement for a designer of engraving and decoration at Christiania Glassmagasin and Hadeland Glassworks. This was in 1954. Before long, she became fascinated by glass as a material to express form and shape. The fairly sober Scandinavian style was at that time still rather prominent, but she had a strong desire to try new ways and to use more vigorous and rustic forms and colors. When the products she designed came on the market and were also shown in a small exhibition, great public interest was stimulated.

After several years at the large Hadeland factory, Mrs. Motzfeldt started work in a smaller operation where she was in charge of artistic design and produced art glass in single pieces as well as in series. Recently, she joined the Plus Organization (an art craft center) that comes under Norway Designs Export A/S. Here she is in charge of a small glass hut with three blowers, and has the best possible opportunity for production on a purely studio basis and for completely genuine handmade glass. Per Tannum, the director of Norway Designs, has given her a free hand as leader of production at the glass hut in Frederikstad. (See Color Plate 112.)

"I live with the glass material, and to form it and to express myself through it is my main interest," says Mrs. Motzfeldt. "I try to work without marked influence from others or from trends in style and form. I think one's products should be an expression of what one feels and wishes to express as a member of today's and tomorrow's society. If it is personal, genuine, and true, I hope others will understand and appreciate it."

Acknowledged today as one of the leading exponents of Norwegian glass art, this fine artist has built up a reputation that is recognized internationally. She has had a great number of one-man exhibitions both at home and abroad, as well as participating in joint exhibitions arranged by Norwegian authorities and institutions. Criticisms and reviews of her work have been positive and appreciative. Not long ago, the town of Bergen celebrated its 900th anniversary, and as part of the celebration Mrs. Motzfeldt was invited to stage a one-man show in the Vestlandske Kunstindustrimuseet. In May 1971, she held a similar exhibition in the Kunstindustrimuseet in Copenhagen, Denmark.

Following here are a number of short excerpts from press reviews and criticisms of Benny Motzfeldt's work:

> We here witness the fine cooperation between the craftsman and the designer. Together they realize the intentions inherent in the sketches, allow the material and the creative process to combine in determining the final result—a unique work of art in glittering glass. The works may resemble one another, have a mutual kinship, but each one is distinctive and individual.

> In Benny Motzfeldt's case, the inquiring compulsion is given expression by an imagination that is quite without equal in Norwegian glass-art. Created with a fertile, pulsating fantasy and in continually changing styles, Benny Motzfeldt's excellent products have . . . created some confusion in the glass producers' and traders' beautiful ranks of traditional and unadventurous decorative glass.

> The artist has obviously thrown the old conventions overboard as to how glass is supposed to look and what glass is to be used for, and has felt free to undertake an extensive study of the possibilities of glass, with regard also to decorative expression. Here one finds bubbles, infused metals, mat and transparent glass together and apart, both in wealth of colors. But Mrs. Motzfeldt's works are free of the unpleasant slipperiness or the rough baroque exterior that many glass artists cultivate. This positive quality is, I feel, due not

235. Benny Motzfeldt, Norway. 4½". Signed "B.M.—Benny Motzfeldt, 1971"

only to a well-founded technical knowledge, but also to a very sensitive understanding of the significance of the form.

  We do not find . . . many workers in glass, and again it is Benny Motzfeldt who emerges from the first rank, exhibiting her works from her new glass hut at Plus. Benny Motzfeldt possesses an apparently unbounded fantasy where the material, glass, and its possibilities are concerned, not least in respect to daring colors, and she never succumbs to loose inventions.

  Benny Motzfeldt's work in Norwegian glass production has in many ways had a regenerative effect, and her creative abilities have resulted in an often unusual understanding of the decorative possibilities of glass. [She] is engaged in developing this tendency as a loner in our domestic scene.

237.
Benny Motzfeldt, Norway. 6¼". Signed
"Benny Motzfeldt, Plus, Norway"

236.
Benny Motzfeldt, Norway. 10½". Signed
"Benny Motzfeldt, 1971"

239.
Benny Motzfeldt, Norway. 8". Signed
"Benny Motzfeldt, 1971"

◀238.
Benny Motzfeldt, Norway. 7". Signed
"Benny Motzfeldt, 1971"

240–241–242.
Benny Motzfeldt, Norway. *(Left)* 5¼". Signed "Benny Motzfeldt." *(Center)* 2½". Signed "Benny Motzfeldt, 1971." *(Right)* 4½". Signed "Benny Motzfeldt, B.M. '71."

SWEDEN

AFORS GLASS FACTORY

This factory was started in 1876 by the brothers Carl, Oskar, and Alfred Fagerlund and a relative, Karl Karlsson. All of them were master glass craftsmen from the Kosta works. About 1880, Carl Fagerlund became sole owner. In 1911, together with his children, he formed Aktiebolaget Afors Glassbruk.

Ernst Johansson, a wholesale dealer, bought the factory in 1917. His son Erik Afors took over the management two years after that, and thereafter was the top executive. The production has, over the subsequent years, been varied—including, among other items, restaurant glass, pressed glass, stem and barware glass, art and household glass in crystal and potash with cut, painted, engraved, etched, and blasted decor. Today's products are completely blown by mouth (handmade). Since the beginning of 1960, Bertil Vallien has been artist and designer at the factory.

In 1935 Erik Afors bought 50 percent of the shares in the Kosta glassworks; these holdings later were increased to 67 percent, and in 1947 the Boda glass factory was bought. This was the beginning of the cooperation between Afors, Kosta, Boda, and Johannesfors glassworks that prevailed during the 1960s. Since 1971 these factories have belonged to a combine called AB Aforsgruppen, with Erik Rosen as managing director.

BERTIL VALLIEN

B. Vallien

B. Vallien

Bertil Vallien was born in 1938. After being an honor student at Sweden's State School of Arts, Crafts, and Design, he was awarded a Royal Scholarship for study in the United States. At that time he worked exclusively with ceramics. Deciding to take a chance, Vallien entered the competition "Young Americans"—and won. Next he took part in the biennial exhibition at the Everton Museum of Arts in New York, and received first prize.

Vallien stayed in America two years before returning to Sweden, where Erik Rosen at Boda soon got hold of him. With enormous enthusiasm Vallien at once threw himself into working with the new materials that the craftsmen in Smaland put before him: glass, wrought iron, and wood. He experimented wildly with colors and forms, and since cutting and etching did not entirely satisfy his need to express himself, he used sandblasting in order to work deeper into the glass and achieve new effects and contrasts. There is a kind of designer's joy in Bertil Vallien's pieces, a billowing, swelling rhythm. But he has not forgotten ceramics—he shares with his wife, Ulrika, who also works in clay sculptures, a private workshop near the glass foundry. (See Color Plate 114.)

243.
Bertil Vallien, Sweden. 11¾". Signed "Boda-Afors, Unik 1627—B. Vallien, 1970"

244.
Bertil Vallien, Sweden. 6¾". Signed "Boda-Afors, Unik 1625, B. Vallien, 1970"

245.
Bertil Vallien, Sweden. 3¼". Signed "Boda-Afors, Unik 929, B. Vallien, 1970"

246. Bertil Vallien, Sweden. 7¾". Signed "Boda-Afors, Unik 1626, B. Vallien, 1970"

247. Bertil Vallien, Sweden. 4½". Signed "Boda-Afors, Unik 779, B. Vallien, 1970.

Boda

Printed in Sweden by Johansson & Svenson

BODA GLASSWORKS—SWEDEN

There is a province in south Sweden named Smaland (literally, "little land"). It is a barren and rugged region with an oversupply of stones and rocks and deep woods that cover square mile upon square mile. Parts of Smaland where the forests are dense but the inhabitants few are often referred to by other Swedes as "darkest Smaland." Here is where one finds many of the glassworks that have made Swedish glass and Swedish design famous among experts and art lovers all over the world.

It is primarily due to the forests that glassworks are to be found in this region. The never-ending fuel resources were an important factor in locating the factories there, once the art of glassmaking finally reached the Nordic countries some three hundred years ago. Today, such plants can be established anywhere, since modern furnaces use oil as fuel and import raw materials from around the world, wherever the highest quality is to be found. Smaland proved to be an ideal location for another reason also, however: the men and women in this province, to whom nature has granted few material assets, seem to have—as compensation—more imagination and enterprise, a sound business sense, and almost stubborn determination. Undoubtedly, they have always had to make the most of what they had, and they readily adapted the skill they developed in centuries of working with wood and iron to working with glass and crystal. Today, they are second to none in the art of shaping the glowing glass mass into useful goods or decorative articles of glistening elegance, using simple tools the Phoenicians invented 2,000 years ago.

The past is not of much concern at Boda Glassworks, one of the factories in this part of Sweden. The plant has twice burned down, so there is—after all—not much to look back on. The present and the future are more important. It is only during the last ten years or so that Boda has grown into one of the largest art-glass works in Sweden and gained a leading position for its designs and new ideas. Erik Rosen, the managing director (for AB Aforsgruppen, of which Boda is a part), and his teams of designers and workers are complete individualists with firm standards and great artistic awareness.

The oldest Swedish glassworks have kept their furnaces burning for more than two hundred years. Boda, only one hundred years old, is hardly more than a youngster in such company, but it was founded by veteran glassblowing masters and so has had the benefit of a professional tradition from the beginning. Equally important, though, is its strong ambition to choose its own ways, to create its own success. Although Boda has outgrown its baby clothes and come of age, it still cherishes a young outlook, a spirit of competition, and the boldness of youth. With these assets unimpaired, the future stretches challengingly ahead.

MONICA BOCKSTROM

Monica Bockstrom, who comes from a Stockholm family with a heritage of artistic recognition, has been with Boda Glassworks for several years. Her personal artistic ability and her delight in glass as a material are very evident, and she produces highly individual work that portends a promising future for her as a designer. (See Color Plate 111.)

Monica Bockström

248.
Monica Bockstrom, Sweden. 5″. Signed "M.B. 4785, Unik, Monica Bockstrom, Kosmos, 20–8–70"

Erik Höglund

ERIK S. HOGLUND

Sculptor Erik S. Hoglund, born in 1932 in Karlskrona, studied at the School of Industrial Art in Stockholm from 1948 to 1953. He won the Lunning Prize in 1958; later he traveled on scholarships to Greece, Italy, Spain, France, Switzerland, the United States, Mexico, and Guatemala. From 1953 on, he also has worked as a designer at Boda Glassworks.

Hoglund is represented at the National Museum in Stockholm and in many museums elsewhere in Sweden and in other countries. He has created sculptures in cast bronze for various Swedish cities: Trelleborg, Boras, Stockholm, Karlskoga, Sandviken, and Vaxjo. He has also made decorative windows in "mural glass" for the cathedral in Vaxjo, the church at Lessebo, Slottsstadens Church in Malmo, the town hall in Eskilstuna, the Sjobo School in Boras, the Svenska Handelsbanken in Stockholm-Oskarshamm-Vimmerby, the Norra Kavaljeren Restaurant in Halmstad, the Rode Orm Restaurant in Gothenburg, and the Funkabo School in Kalmar-Johannelund-Linkoping. In addition, he has designed church doors in copper plates for the church in Madesjo and doors in wrought brass for the Lorensberg Restaurant in Gothenburg.

249.
Erik Hoglund, Sweden. 7″. Signed "10. Swedish glass, Erik Hoglund, made 23–8–70"

Basically, Erik Hoglund is a sculptor. Some years ago when he was quite young, however, he had the opportunity of working with glass. He succeeded so well that he celebrated his tenth anniversary as a glass designer at the Boda Glassworks in 1964, simultaneously with the firm's one-hundredth anniversary. To the connoisseur of glass Hoglund is well known today—many consider him a "renewer" of the art of glassmaking in Sweden. He has a primitive grasp that is a refreshing contrast to the polished achievements of many others.

Hoglund thinks that glass is beautiful in itself and so takes full advantage of all its basic qualities: bubbles, refraction, color. His glass for domestic use has always had a very personal touch, even when produced in larger series. At exhibits, an important position is often given to his decorative creations in "mural glass," which can be assembled in big shimmering walls such as are often used in churches and public buildings. His sculptured glass—heads framed in iron or mounted on rods—has an unusual decorative quality and is much admired.

It was by coincidence—when he passed the sooty establishment of a smith one day—that Hoglund became interested in wrought iron. He first started, as with so many other things, by "playing" with the new material. Today his chandeliers and candelabra of wrought iron with hanging glass medallions give occupation to many ironsmiths. The contrast between the sooty-dark iron and sparkling glass has been developed by Hoglund for a variety of decorative purposes.

Hoglund also makes furniture for children's rooms. First, he made furniture for his own children, but it soon became so renowned that it grew into a production item. Other wooden articles like candlesticks, bowls, and plates give added proof of his ability to use a material in his own special way, once he has taken an interest in it. His is a creative mind that attacks each new challenge with fresh enthusiasm.

During his more than ten years at Boda, Hoglund has not secluded himself in a house of glass. He keeps constantly and completely aware of everything that goes on around him there and in the world at large, and so is always discovering new possibilities, new materials, new objects that stimulate his creativity. But, at the same time, he continues the work for which he was trained initially—the art of sculpture. (See also Color Plate 109.)

250. ▶
Erik Hoglund, Sweden. 8¼". Signed "Erik Hoglund, Boda, 25–8–1970"

◀251.
Erik Hoglund, Sweden. 12". Signed "Empty twin bottles, Erik Hoglund, 25–8–1970"

252.
Erik Hoglund, Sweden. 10″. Signed "4. Jug torso, Erik Hoglund, Boda, 25–8–1970"

253.
Erik Hoglund, Sweden. 12¼″. Signed "A sleeping glass, Erik Hoglund, Boda, 25–8–70"

254–255–256.
Erik Hoglund, Sweden. *(Left)* 4″. Signed "Jug (emptied), Erik Hoglund, Boda, 25–8–1970." *(Center)* 4¼″. Signed "Living jug, Erik Hoglund, 25–8–1970." *(Right)* 6½″. Signed "Movement at 260°, Erik Hoglund, 25–8–1970"

KOSTA GLASSWORKS

For more than 225 years since its founding in 1742, the Kosta Glassworks has been renowned. Located in the midst of the forests of south Sweden, Kosta was begun by two Swedish noblemen, Generals Anders Koskull and Georg Bogislaus Stael von Holstern, who also gave the name to the factory: KO from Koskull and STA from Stael von Holstern.

Kosta is the oldest still-working glass manufactory in Sweden producing table glassware and fancy articles. During the first period Kosta produced window glass, drinking sets, and chandeliers of glass, of which some original samples from the very first period may still be seen in churches in the neighborhood.

Transportation of glass was a great problem at that time. Hardly any roads existed, and from Kosta to the port of Kalmar was a journey of four days although the distance was only about fifty miles. The glass was packed in straw and sent there in oxcarts. From Kalmar it might be shipped, for instance, to Stockholm, but many salesmen also went out on foot to visit the farms and sell directly.

Glassblowers were held in high esteem and had numerous privileges. In their contract it was stipulated that a glassblower had the right to have a riding horse and could wear a braid in his hat. And when a master blower attended a "treat" the peasantry had to wear their festival attire.

From the beginning there was an ardent desire at Kosta to develop the plant, and over the years the management has always worked toward that end. With the help of capable hands, a solid tradition and a fine name have been built up.

Around 1800, English clubs started to use sets of glasses decorated with the club emblem, and these were probably the first that Kosta made of what one calls "wine services" today. They have excelled for more than 150 years in producing beautiful wine sets, from the well-shaped but comparatively simple type to the most intricate and richly decorated ones.

Skilled workers and talented designers are the necessary combination for successful glassmaking. Kosta employed its first designer in 1898: Gunnar G-son Wennerberg, son of the well-known poet with the same name. The design staff in Kosta presently includes Vicke Lindstrand, Mona Morales-Schildt, and Ann and Goran Warff.

Today Kosta works incessantly, not only to uphold its tradition but above all to meet the demands of continuous progress. New techniques are eagerly explored; the artists frequently create new designs that necessitate experimenting with different methods of production, but the staff responds to such challenges.

Glass for everyday use as well as beautiful pieces of art continues to be shipped all over the world from Kosta, adding continually to the firm's outstanding reputation.

Bengt Heintze (born 1905), master glassblower at Kosta.

VICKE LINDSTRAND

Vicke Lindstrand was born in 1904 in Gothenburg. He attended the School of the Swedish Society of Arts and Crafts there and—greatly interested in music—became first soloist and organist in the German Church in Gothenburg. For several years this talented man was also editor of the *Gotesborgs Handels- & Sjofartstidning* and the *Gotesborgs-Tidningen*, and was an extremely capable cartoonist as well.

Lindstrand started working in glass in 1928 when he began as a designer at Orrefors Glassworks. In the following decade he participated in many national and international exhibits: the Triennale in Milan, 1933, the world exhibit in Paris in 1937, and in New York in 1939, as well as several exhibitions in Sweden.

In 1940 Lindstrand started a new activity when he went to the Upsala-Ekeby China Manufactory, where he remained until 1950. At Upsala-Ekeby there was a vast field for the exercise of his talents, and he developed many interesting ideas in ceramics.

Lindstrand went to work at Kosta in 1950 as a designer and the director of design. He has worked there with a great variety of new ideas, often in combination with new techniques. In the years since he has been associated with Kosta, Lindstrand has had a number of special exhibits: Stockholm in 1951, Copenhagen in 1953, London in 1954, and Gothenburg in 1956, to name a few. He has also participated in many Kosta exhibits—for instance, "H–55" (Halsingborg 1955), Stockholm 1957, New York 1957, Dusseldorf 1958, Lund 1959, Hamburg (Museum fur Kunst und Gewerbe) 1960, Nordiska Museet in Stockholm 1960, and New York 1960.

The artistic variety of Vicke Lindstrand's work is amazing. He understands the latent possibilities of thick, undulating glass, and combines and adapts the Graal and Ariel techniques with great inventiveness and elegant artistry. (See Color Plate 115.)

MONA MORALES-SCHILDT

Mona Morales-Schildt comes from a family of artists. Her father was a composer and conductor and her mother a singer and voice teacher. Instead of taking up music, Mona Schildt was attracted by the visual and sculptural components in art.

She began her training at the School of Industrial Art; next came scholarships for the study of china in England and Germany. She also studied painting in Paris. In 1936 she took a position at Gustavsberg as assistant to Wilhelm Kage. The year 1939 saw her employed by the Arabia porcelain factory in Finland—until the war began. Returning to Stockholm, she managed the new Gustavsberg shop until 1941, when she married the author Goran Schildt.

From 1945 to 1957 Mona Morales-Schildt worked for Nordiska Kompaniet in Stockholm, where she was in charge of the arrangements in the decorative arts section and the exhibits there. Since 1958, she has been employed as a designer at the Kosta glassworks, but has had her own exhibits at Nordiska Kompaniet in Stockholm, Artium in Gothenburg, and Artek in Helsingfors, and also in Munich. She participated in the Kosta exhibits in Lund's Konsthall in 1959, Nordiska Museet in Stockholm in 1960, Museum fur Kunst und Gewerbe in Hamburg in 1960, and in New York, 1961. (See Color Plate 118.)

Glass designed by Mrs. Morales-Schildt is exhibited at the National Museum in Hamburg and the Corning Museum of Glass in the United States.

257. Mona Morales-Schildt, Sweden. 11¼". Signed "Kosta, 1969, Mona Morales-Schildt, 5–423"

Rolf Sinnemark

ROLF SINNEMARK

Rolf Sinnemark was born in 1941. He took courses in industrial design at the Swedish State School of Arts and Design. In 1965/66 he was Sweden-America Foundation Scholar in Denver, Colorado, and he has also traveled for study in Mexico, Greece, Italy, and France. Sinnemark has been a designer at Kosta since 1967. (See Color Plate 113.)

258.
Rolf Sinnemark, Sweden. 3¾″. Signed "Kosta, Unik, R. Sinnemark, 1970"

GORAN WARFF

Born on the island of Gotland, 1933

After studying architecture and design in Brunswick and Ulm, in 1959 Goran Warff became a designer at the Pukebergs Glassworks, where he remained until 1964. Then he and his wife Ann joined the Kosta glassworks, where they work together on their designs and projects. In fact, their pieces of glass are jointly signed, for there is no junior member in this partnership. Since they keep the same working hours, they have a housekeeper to take care of their children in their nearby home during the day.

Mr. and Mrs. Warff exhibited jointly at "Form Fantasi" in 1964, Rohnska Museet in 1965, and N.K. in 1968. They were joint winners of the Lunning Prize in 1968 as well. The Warffs are represented at the National Museum in Stockholm, the Corning Museum of Glass in the United States, and the Pilkington Museum in England.

ANN WARFF

Born in Lubeck, 1937

After studying graphics in Hamburg, Ulm, and Zurich, Ann Schaefer married Goran Warff and joined Pukebergs Glassworks in 1960. In 1963 she published a children's book, *Plimse,* and in 1964, along with her husband, joined the Kosta firm.

As indicated in the preceding text on Goran Warff, this husband-and-wife team works together; sometimes they do have individual projects, but they usually work in the same direction. Even in overseeing their master glassblower, they function as equal partners.

The future of the Warffs in the Swedish glass industry should not be underestimated. Originality of design and insistence on technical perfection are the prerequisites for recognition everywhere, and the Warffs are known for these qualities.

259. Ann and Goran Warff, Sweden. 5½". Signed "Ann and Goran Warff"

260. Ann and Goran Warff, Sweden. 4¼". Signed "Kosta 740, 1968, Ann and Goran Warff"

261.
Ann and Goran Warff, Sweden.
4″. Signed "Ann and Goran
Warff, Kosta, 1967, Kosta-Warff,
V–198"

262.
Ann and Goran Warff, Sweden.
2½″. Signed "Kosta-Unik 692,
Ann and Goran Warff, 1969"

263.
Ann and Goran Warff, Sweden. 3½″. Signed
"Kosta 722B, 1970, Ann and Goran Warff"

264.
Ann and Goran Warff, Sweden. 6¾″. Signed
"Kosta, 96789, Warff, 1969, Ann and Goran
Warff"

265.
Ann and Goran Warff, Sweden. 3″.
Signed "Kosta 7134, 1970, Ann and Goran Warff"

ORREFORS GLASSWORKS

Orrefors was founded in 1726 as an ironworks, for which the ore was gathered from the lake bottoms. In the course of time this industry became less profitable, and Orrefors adapted itself to a different production. Today this factory, which is located in the province of Smaland amid the great forests, has a worldwide reputation for creating beautiful glass—sometimes romantic and sometimes massive and robust.

In 1898 Orrefors was making ink bottles and window glass. In 1913 Consul Johan Ekman of Gothenburg bought a tract of forest in Smaland for his cellulose plant, and Orrefors was included in the purchase. After a few years under the new ownership, rapid and eventful progress began to be made and Orrefors acquired a

broader reputation. Now, under the direction of Johan Beyer, it is heavily committed to the production of unique pieces of glass.

The continuing success of the Orrefors glassworks stems from the freedom it gives its creative staff. The designers work closely with the master craftsman and his supporting artisans, and it is this close teamwork that makes possible the very fine quality of Orrefors glassware: pieces with a distinctive individuality—truly faultless works of art.

GUNNAR CYREN

Gunnar Cyren has been working at Orrefors since 1959. He trained originally to be a silversmith, and after completing his studies at the Swedish State School of Arts, he at first devoted his attention to stainless steel, silver, and gold. He won the Lunning Prize in 1966.

The glass of Gunnar Cyren reveals an incredible amount of detail and manual finesse. It is all brightness and shimmer, with great freshness and originality. (See Color Plate 120.)

NILS LANDBERG

Nils Landberg, a designer whose work is marked by great elegance, came to Orrefors in 1925. He works with hand-blown as well as engraved glass, and is represented in major museums in Sweden and around the world. Landberg won a gold medal at the 1957 Triennale. (See Color Plate 120.)

INGEBORG LUNDIN

Ingeborg Lundin has been employed at Orrefors since 1947. She studied at the Swedish State School of Arts.

    The 1954 Lunning Prize and a gold medal at the 1957 Triennale are just two of the awards this glass artist has received. Miss Lundin's glass shapes are clear and simple. She works with a natural spontaneity, and all her glass has lightness, movement, and grace. Her glass vessels are usually of the utmost simplicity with pure lines and only one or two colors. (See Color Plate 123.)

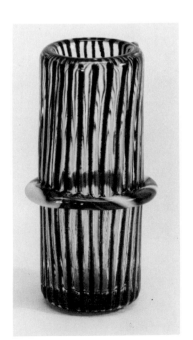

266. Ingeborg Lundin, Sweden. 7¼". Signed "Orrefors-Graal 452–70, Ingeborg Lundin"

267.
Ingeborg Lundin, Sweden. 3½″. Signed "Orrefors, Ariel 430–68, Ingeborg Lundin"

268.
Ingeborg Lundin, Sweden. 6″. Signed "Orrefors-Graal 467–70, Ingeborg Lundin"

269.
Ingeborg Lundin, Sweden. 7″. Signed "Orrefors-Graal, N.Y. 464–70, Ingeborg Lundin"

270. ▶
Ingeborg Lundin, Sweden. 6½″. Signed "Orrefors-Graal 466–70, Ingeborg Lundin"

271.
Ingeborg Lundin, Sweden. 4¼″. Signed "Orrefors-Graal 314–67, Ingeborg Lundin"

272. ▶
Ingeborg Lundin, Sweden. 7½″. Signed "Orrefors-Graal 465–70, Ingeborg Lundin"

Plate 103.   Tapio Wirkkala, Italy. Piece in center, 9 inches.

Plate 104.   Aureliano Toso, Italy. 6¼ inches.

Plate 105.   Willy Johansson, Norway. 7½ inches.

Plate 106.   Santillana-Venini, Italy. Bottle, 15 inches.

Plate 107. Giancarlo Begotti, Italy. 16¾ inches.
Signed "Giancarlo Begotti '58"

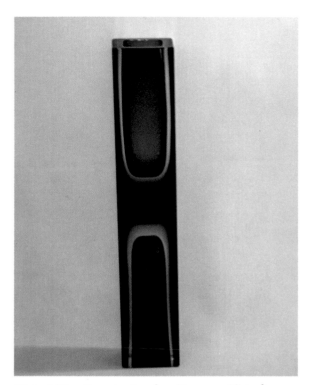

Plate 108. Severin Brorby, Norway. 10 inches.

Plate 109. Erik Hoglund, Sweden. 8 inches.
Signed "Erik Hoglund, Boda 25–8–1970, Mother
and Two Children"

Plate 110. Gro Sommerfelt, Norway. 13 inches.
Signed "Hadeland, Norway, Gro Sommerfelt"

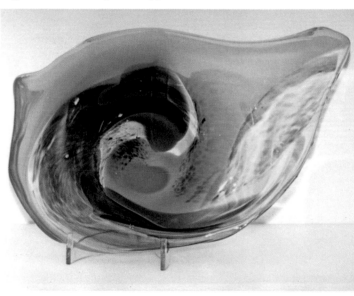

Plate 111. Monica Bockstrom, Sweden. 10¼ inches. "Monica Bockstrom, Fallos D–20–8–70, Unik"

Plate 112. Benny Motzfeldt, Norway. 6¾ inches. Signed "BM70—Benny Motzfeldt 1971"

Plate 113. Rolf Sinnemark, Sweden. 7½ inches. Signed "Kosta 76250, Sinnemark 1969"

Plate 114. Bertil Vallien, Sweden. 4¾ inches. Signed "Boda-Afors-Unik, B. Vallien, 1970"

Plate 115. Vicke Lindstrand, Sweden. 5¼ inches. Signed "Kosta, Lindstrand 1970"

Plate 116. Ann and Goran Warff, Sweden. 7½ inches. Signed "Kosta 739, 1968, Ann & Goran Warff"

Plate 117. Ann and Goran Warff, Sweden. 3¾ inches. Signed "Kosta 1970/105, Ann & Goran Warff"

Plate 118. Mona Morales-Schildt, Sweden. 7¼ inches. Signed "Kosta, M. Morales 1970"

Plate 119. Eva Englund, Sweden. 5½ and 5¾ inches.

Plate 120. Cyren and Landberg, Sweden. 8¼ and 17½ inches.

Plate 121. Bengt Edenfalk, Sweden. 5¾ inches.

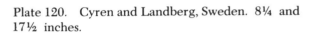

Plate 122. Eva Englund, Sweden. 7 inches.

Plate 123. Ingeborg Lundin, Sweden. 5½ inches. Signed "Orrefors D.306–67, Ingebord Lundin"

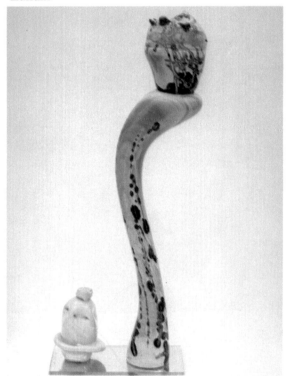

Plate 124. Erwin Eisch, West Germany. 22¾ inches. Signed "E. Eisch, 1971"

Plate 125. Sven Palmquist, Sweden. 4½ inches. Signed "Orrefors, Ravenna, 4669, Sven Palmquist"

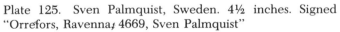

Plate 126. Edvin Ohrstrom, Sweden. 8 and 8½ inches.

Plate 127. Erwin Eisch, West Germany. 17 inches. Signed "E. Eisch, 1971"

Plate 128. Professor Konrad Habermeier, West Germany. 9¼ and 5 inches.

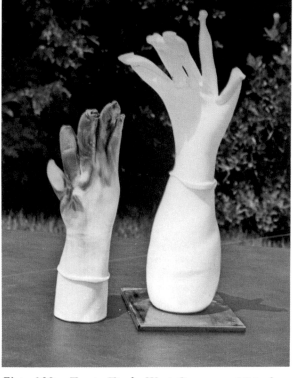

Plate 129. Erwin Eisch, West Germany. 13 inches. Signed "E. Eisch, 1971"

Plate 130. Karl Wiedmann, West Germany. 7½ inches. Signed "Design—Karl Wiedmann Gral-Glas, Durnau 1971"

Plate 131. Gunther Hofmann, West Germany. 9½ inches.

Plate 132. Max Gangkofner, West Germany. 5 inches.

Plate 133. Helmut Rotter, West Germany. 5 inches. Signed "Franz von Liszt, Helmut Rotter, 1967"

Plate 134. Bernhard Schagemann, West Germany. 7¾ inches. Signed "Fachschule, Zwiesel, 1968, B. Schagemann"

Plate 135. Raoul Goldoni, Yugoslavia. 9½ inches. Signed "R. Goldoni–A. Barbini"

EDVIN OHRSTROM

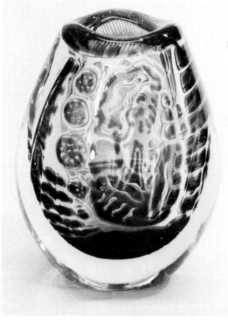

273.
Edvin Ohrstrom, Sweden. 8". Signed "Orrefors, Ariel 427, Edvin Ohrstrom"

Edvin Ohrstrom is a sculptor and glass designer. For many years he has made attractive glassware for everyday use, as well as exquisite ornamental glass for the connoisseur, at the Orrefors glassworks. It is said of him: "With creative imagination and deep feeling for the potentialities of the material, he was one of those who helped to build up the international reputation of Swedish glass and to make the name of Orrefors known throughout the world."

Today Ohrstrom concerns himself entirely with independent colored-glass sculptures, which have great vitality, a robust primitive power and strength. His works of art in glass are compositions of color and decorative exuberance. (See Color Plate 126.)

SVEN PALMQUIST

After graduating from the Technical College, Academy of Fine Arts in Stockholm and the College of Art in Paris, where he was taught by Paul Cornet, Sven Palmquist went to Orrefors in 1928.

Known for his art glass and the monumental decorative work he has done for public buildings in Sweden and elsewhere, Palmquist won the Grand Prix at the 1957 Triennale. His sketches result in delicate classical engravings. He invented the so-called Ravenna glass, used for heavy vessels and usually tinted to produce transparent color with simple inlaid patterns. (See Color Plate 125.)

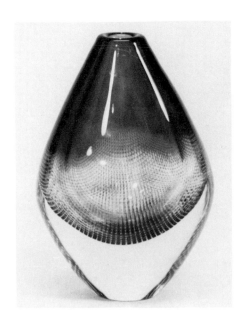

274.
Sven Palmquist, Sweden. 8½″. Signed "Orrefors, Kraka 349, Sven Palmquist"

275.
Sven Palmquist, Sweden. 5¼″. Signed "Orrefors, Kraka 479, Sven Palmquist"

PUKEBERGS GLASSWORKS

Pukebergs Glassworks, founded in 1871, is situated in the glass district of Smaland, two kilometers southeast of the center of Nybro City. It has kept pace with the times and is now a modern plant with up-to-date technical equipment and a steady trend toward expansion.

The production at this glassworks consists mainly of lighting fixtures and illuminating glassware, but Pukebergs has also created a line of modern domestic and ornamental glassware. Over the years, as the firm has developed, it has earned a place among the leading manufacturers of artist-designed glass and of lighting fixtures for modern homes and public buildings. Besides the designers directly associated with the company, other designers both in Sweden and abroad also collaborate in the production.

EVA ENGLUND

Eva Englund was born in 1937. She passed examinations at the art school, Konstfack, in Stockholm, and also studied at the Kunstakademie in Munich. In 1959 she became a designer at the Schleiss pottery factory in Austria. This charming artist, who has one son (Luv), teaches at the Carl Malmsten School. In 1964 she also became associated with Pukebergs Glassworks, where she mainly designs household and fancy glasses.

Eva Englund has had special exhibitions at the following museums: 1965 at Hoganas; 1966, Vaxjo; 1967, Kalmar; 1968, Varberg; 1970–1971, Liljevalchs, Stockholm; 1971, Vaxjo, Norriviken, Bastad, and "Form," Malmo. She is also represented at the National Museum in Stockholm, the Smalands Museum in Vaxjo, and Kalmar Museum in Kalmar. Today she is recognized as one of the outstanding originators of youthful Swedish designs. (See Color Plate 122.)

276. Eva Englund, Sweden. 16″.
Signed "Eva Englund, 1971"

278.
Eva Englund, Sweden. 7½″.
Signed "Eva Englund, 1971"

◄277.
Eva Englund, Sweden. 4½″.
Signed "Eva Englund, 1971"

SKRUF GLASSWORKS

In the parish of Ljuder in Smaland, Sweden, is located the Skruf Glassworks. The first melting at this factory took place in April 1897. In the years since then, the works have survived many vicissitudes and changed ownership several times.

  The present owner, Ernst Karlson, took over in 1930. Under his far-sighted direction progress has been steady and the firm has gained constantly increasing esteem. To assist him, for some years he has attracted to his staff a number of much younger men. Today, Skruf, considered to be one of the leading glassworks in Sweden, continues its good progress.

BENGT EDENFALK

279.
Bengt Edenfalk, Sweden. 5″.
Signed "Bengt Edenfalk, Skruf"

280.
Bengt Edenfalk, Sweden. 8½″.
Signed "Bengt Edenfalk, Skruf,
Thelatta"

Bengt Edenfalk was employed as a designer by Skruf Glassworks in 1953.

Edenfalk has achieved success in both Swedish and foreign competitions. Among exhibitions where his work has attracted favorable attention are the following: Swedish Design Cavalcade in U.S.A., Form I Centrum, 1958; "Glass," international exhibition at the Corning Glass Center, 1959, where he was one of the leading names; and the Triennales in Milan. He was one of the first-prize winners in a competition for the adornment of the T-Centralen (tube station) in Stockholm. Aside from his work as a designer, Bengt Edenfalk has made several large walls in Italian mosaic. (See Color Plate 121.)

WEST GERMANY

ERWIN EISCH

GLASHÜTTE
VALENTIN EISCH KG
FRAUENAU
BAYERISCHER WALD

Erwin Eisch stems from an old Bavarian family of glass engravers. Born on April 18, 1927, in Frauenau in the Bavarian forest of West Germany, he trained as an engraver and then attended the Munich Academy of Art, where he studied industrial design, painting, and sculpture. Since then, he has earned international recognition in three fields—as an artist, sculptor, and glassblower. In 1957, Eisch married Gretl Stadler, who is a most hospitable and capable wife.

Eisch's work admirably documents his thorough understanding of glass as a medium—he reaches into the realm of poetry and fantasy, beyond the functional into

Erwin Eisch

pure creativity. His pieces are also unusual in that he creates them without needing technical help, for he has developed all the skills needed for working glass on his own. To him, as to most other glassmakers, there is an irresistible challenge to the process of forming objects from molten glass in the brief time he controls it before it cools and hardens.

In 1957, when Harvey Littleton, the American artist, potter, glassblower, and industrial designer, was investigating the possibility of opening a studio-glass department at the University of Wisconsin, he discovered the work of Erwin Eisch. So impressed was he with this work done in Frauenau that he persuaded Eisch to spend six weeks in the United States helping to set up the new department and serving as guest instructor. Eisch has also taught at San Jose State College in California.

The factory in Frauenau was built by the Eisch family—the father Valentien, a noted engraver, and brothers Erich and Alphons. Erwin served as designer and one

281.
Erwin Eisch, West Germany. 11¾".
Signed "E. Eisch, 1965"

282. ▲
Erwin Eisch, West Germany. 6¼".
Signed "E. Eisch, 1971"

283. ▶
Erwin Eisch, West Germany. 4½".
Signed "E. Eisch, 1971"

284.
Erwin Eisch, West Germany. 5½".
Signed "E. Eisch, 1971"

◀285.
Erwin Eisch, West Germany. 11½".
Signed "E. Eisch, 1965"

286. ▶
Erwin Eisch, West Germany. 10¼".
Signed "E. Eisch, 1971"

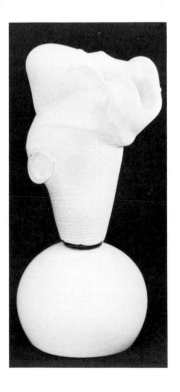

of his brothers as director. Today the original factory is Erwin Eisch's home and studio, and a new and larger factory has been built adjacent to it. Erwin sometimes works with an assistant, Karl Paternoster, and his brother-in-law as a team.

Harvey Littleton has called Eisch a "maverick" whose reputation is greater in the United States, where original hand-blown glass is now appreciated more than it is in Germany. To Eisch himself, the activity of glassblowing is a magical, enchanting performance. He says about his work: "From a glowing inert mass must emerge things of beauty that are endowed with speech. A talent of innovating, creating animatedly, and the breath to blow are requisites. Without blowing nothing happens." Clearly, Eisch combines the skill of an industrial designer with the sensitivity of an expressionistic artist; but, as an artist, his work is strictly personal. (See Color Plates 124, 127, and 129.)

Today, through the farseeing eyes of Harvey Littleton and Erwin Eisch, the way has been opened up to bring the student of glass design into much closer contact with the material he is using. It would also seem that glass artists like these two have rendered a service to industry and to the public as well by stimulating the appreciation of glass as an artistic medium.

The glasshouse at Frauenau engages in craft production rather than following the current trend toward mechanization. Works of Erwin Eisch are in the following private and permanent collections:

Corning Museum, Corning, New York

Elvium Art Centre, Madison, Wisconsin

Landesmuseum, Oldenburg, West Germany

Museum Boymans-Van Beuningen, Rotterdam, The Netherlands

Museum fur Kunst und Gewerbe, Hamburg, West Germany

Sammlung Veste, Coburg, West Germany

Smithsonian Institution, Washington, D.C.

Toledo Museum of Art, Toledo, Ohio

287. Erwin Eisch, West Germany. 6½". Signed "E. Eisch, 1971"

288. Erwin Eisch, West Germany. 9½". Signed "E. Eisch, 1971"

GRAL GLASSWORKS

Gral Glassworks of Durnau, West Germany, which is under the management of the co-owner Rolf Seyfang, was founded in 1930. The firm started as a glass refinery, and at first only applied arts and handicraft dealers showed any interest in the severe style of its designs and cut. Several years were needed before this style gained acceptance, but from then on things moved very quickly: the range of products was extended and an export program was formulated.

A subsidiary was set up in the Bohemian Forest in 1938, and in 1939 a glassworks was added to it; owing to the general situation, however, production had to be discontinued. After 1945 it was possible to move more specialist workers from the Bohemian Forest district to Goppingen, thus permitting the establishment of a new glassworks and the increase in production and capacity that was long overdue.

Gral Glassworks has always been a leader in good design, color, and decoration, and these qualities have earned them many awards and commendations. Among the well-known designers who work for Gral, particular mention should be made of Josef Stadler, Professor Konrad Habermeier, Josef Schott, Hermann Schwahn, Kay Krasnitsky, Dr. R. Garnich, and Hans Sukopp. The aim of this team is to produce genuinely artistic designs and decorations, which—although modern in concept—hopefully will prove to be timeless so that owners of Gral crystal can always derive pleasure from it.

Examples of Gral-Glass can be found in German and foreign museums, including the Museum of Modern Art in New York.

KONRAD HABERMEIER

Born in Eyebach, Wurttemberg, 1907

Konrad Habermeier studied and took practical examinations at the Wurttembergischen Metallwarenfabruk in Geislingen, and in Stuttgart; subsequently, he spent further time studying at the Academy of Art in Stuttgart, finally becoming an assistant under Professor Wilhelm Von Eiff. A specialist in glass and stone engraving, cutting, and design, Professor Habermeier currently heads the glass department at the Fachhochschule Swabisch Gmund.

Habermeier is not only regionally known but enjoys an international reputation in his field. Besides being shown at local exhibitions, his work has appeared in the following:

"Glass from Baden-Wurttemberg," Stuttgart, West Germany
"Glass from Four Thousand Years," Zurich, Switzerland

"Good Industrial Form," fairs in Frankfurt, Hanover, Munich, Toronto, and New Delhi

International Glass Exhibition, Corning, New York

"Top Works in Glass," Munich

Triennale, Milan, Italy

"2,000 Years of Glass," Cologne, West Germany

World's Fair, Brussels, Belgium

Articles about Habermeier have appeared in internationally circulated art and trade journals. He received the State Prize in 1964 at Baden-Baden and awards at Frederikshavn in 1959 and Meersburg in 1962. (See Color Plate 128.)

289.
Professor Konrad Habermeier, West Germany. 8½". Signed "Prof. K. Habermeier, Gralglas"

GUNTHER HOFMANN

Born in Zwiesel, Bavaria, April 14, 1940
Wife: Erika, née Muller

From 1946 to 1949 Gunther Hofmann attended the elementary school at Zwiesel, then proceeded to the secondary school at Deggendorf and Zwiesel. In 1955, at fifteen, he started his first apprenticeship as a maker of concave glass at Gral-Glas Hutte Gmbh.; following this, he spent two years as a production glassworker.

From 1960 to 1963, Hofmann attended the Staatliche Hohere Werkkunstschule, where he studied the craft of glass grinding and engraving as well, as a pupil of Professor Konrad Habermeier. He also studied sculpture with Professor Kurt Nuss and design with Professor Karl Dittert. He passed his examinations as a technical engineer for glassworks in 1965, and since then has been employed at Gral-Glas Hutte in Durnau, in southern Germany, where he has been head of the department of design. (See Color Plate 131.)

Günther Hofmann

KARL WIEDMANN

Born in Kuchen Wurttemberg, June 19, 1905

After attending the technical school in applied arts, Wiedmann became an apprentice in glass techniques at Wurttembergischen Metallwarenfabruk ("W.M.F.") in Geislingen: cutting, engraving, grinding, and glassblowing, 1922–24. Two additional years were spent studying at the glass technical school at Zwiesel in Bavaria, before he became technical engineer and manager of the glass department at "W.M.F." His primary creations were in industrial art glass: Myraglas, Ikoraglas, and Lavaluna.

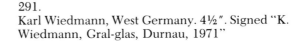

Following the war, during which Wiedmann was imprisoned, he was employed as the technical manager for Daum et Cie in Nancy, France, 1947/48; then he returned to the glass department at "W.M.F." Geislingen, where he served as head from 1948 to 1951. During 1953 and 1954 Wiedmann performed the same function at Farberglaswerke, Zwiesel; from 1954 to 1970 he was the technical director at Gral-Glas, Durnau, prior to his retirement. Corona glass, iris glass, diatreta, and snake-thread glass were Wiedmann innovations. (See Color Plate 130.)

290.
Karl Wiedmann, West Germany. 4″. Signed "K. Wiedmann, 1971, Gral-glas, Durnau"

291.
Karl Wiedmann, West Germany. 4½″. Signed "K. Wiedmann, Gral-glas, Durnau, 1971"

HELMUT ROTTER

Born in Georgswalde, Czechoslovakia, January 13, 1930
Wife: Elsa Brandincuer, 1963
Daughter: Evelin, 1964

With his mother's family in the glass business for many generations, it is not surprising to learn that Helmut Rotter attended the State School for Glass in Haida in 1944, where he concentrated on glass engraving. The war curtailed his studies, and in 1946 he went back home to work in the local glass factory. Evacuated inland along with his family in 1949, he worked on a farm until he was able to get a job in a glass-cutting workshop, first as an engraver, later as a drawer and cutter. From there he returned to Haida, where the technical glass industry was centered, and learned the work of grinding decanters. On May 17, 1953, he and his family fled Czechoslovakia and, after the greatest of difficulties, were able to reach Germany, where he went to work in the glass factory at Immenhausen.

Following six and a half years at Immenhausen and another year at the Gral-Glas factory, he left to spend several years at the Fachhochschule in Schwabisch Gmund. His training there, particularly under the supervision of Professor Habermeier, was particularly important in refining his abilities. After leaving the school with a master's degree, he became self-supporting, working in his own shop.

Rotter is recognized as one of the best European engravers—the quality of his work is outstanding. His pieces are rarely available, being mostly made to order. (See Color Plate 133.)

GOVERNMENT CRAFT and ENGINEERING SCHOOL

Born in Zwiesel, Bayern

In 1904, this school was established in Zwiesel. The small glass companies in the region could take advantage of the training it offered in the technical aspects of glassmaking. The state of Bavaria took over the school in 1906, and improved the whole operation by adding chemical laboratories. After the First World War, so many students from all over Germany began to flock to the school for training in glassmaking that in 1920 a complete expansion of all the facilities was necessary.

Again in 1955, after the Second World War, there was a rebuilding and remodeling program; three enormous furnaces and another structure were added to the compound. In the period between then and 1966, a complete modernization took place so that the most effective methods for the making of glass could be practiced.

The student can learn all the fundamentals here—chemically, technically, and artistically. He can go from the schoolroom with its fine teachers to practical work at the furnaces and in the handling of all glass materials. To receive a diploma requires three years of study. The school is noted in the glass industry for its progress and modernity.

292. Helmut Geib, West Germany. 14¼". Signed "Helmut Geib, F.S. Zwiesel, 1969"

MAX GANGKOFNER

Born in May 16, 1922

Head of the Government Craft and Engineering School in Zwiesel, Max Gangkofner is recognized as a topflight administrator. The many capable and recognized graduates from this school further attest to his ability as a director.

He studied at the Academy of Arts in Munich and taught at the vocational school for glass and jewelry in Gablonz. It was in 1956 that he became associated with the school in Zwiesel. Gracious and cooperative with visitors to the school, he goes out of his way to explain the various available facilities. (See Color Plate 132.)

HANS MAUDER

1903–1970

After graduating from the Academy of Art in Munich, Hans Mauder worked independently in glass finishing until 1931. He taught in Zwiesel from then until his retirement in 1963, during which time—in addition to being an outstanding teacher —he remained involved in glass work.

293.
Hans Mauder, West Germany. 7¾". Signed "Hans Mauder, Fachschule, Zwiesel"

B. Schagemann

BERNHARD SCHAGEMANN

Born in Germany, March 2, 1933

Bernhard Schagemann studied at the Art Academy in Munich. Since 1959 he has created works in glass for religious and other buildings. In 1964 he began teaching a class in designing at the Engineering School in Zwiesel; he is the leader of the Pioneer (trial) Glass Hut. Schagemann has exhibited in various European countries, including Germany, France, and Italy. (See Color Plate 134.)

294.
Bernhard Schagemann, West Germany. 12". Signed "B. Schagemann, 1969"

295. ▶
Bernhard Schagemann, West Germany. 11¼". Signed "1969, B. Schagemann, Zwiesel"

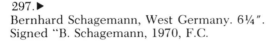

296.
Bernhard Schagemann, West Germany. 4″.
Signed "B. Schagemann, 1968"

297. ▶
Bernhard Schagemann, West Germany. 6¼″.
Signed "B. Schagemann, 1970, F.C."

 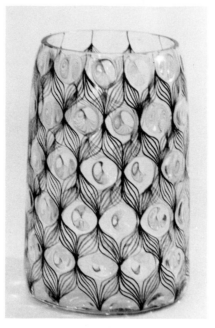

298. Alois Wudy, West Germany. 5½". Signed "Alois Wudy, 1969"

299. Alois Wudy, West Germany. 8¼". Signed "Alois Wudy, 1969"

ALOIS WUDY

Born in Germany, September 12, 1941

With studies in glass, painting, and glassmaking at the government school in Zwiesel, Wudy graduated as a Master Glass Painter, to work in industrial enterprises. Since 1965 he has been head of the department of glass painting at the school in Zwiesel where he studied. His work has been exhibited in Munich, Hamburg, and Stuttgart.

YUGOSLAVIA

RAOUL GOLDONI

Born in Split, Yugoslavia, 1919

This important Yugoslav artist graduated from the Academie des Beaux Arts, Zagreb, in 1942, and took postgraduate studies in Rome. Goldoni is well known in the fields of painting, graphic arts, and book designing. He has also experimented in ceramics, porcelain, and textiles, approaching them from the point of view of art.

His involvement with glass began in 1958, when he became a consultant to several glassworks in Yugoslavia and Italy. Goldoni was particularly at home working

with glass at Alfredo Barbini's furnaces in Murano, where his varied talents could be put into full play. With Barbini he produced many unique pieces of glass with original interpretations.

An important initial step for Goldoni is to lay out an actual drawing of his first idea—an event or scene, perhaps. This original idea may ultimately change on the drawing board into something completely different, and so Goldoni makes a new final sketch prior to starting work on the actual piece of glass. He is a successful combination of artist and glassman and, like Robert Willson and Alfredo Barbini, serious and highly competent, one whose work future collectors will seek out. Unfortunately his output is limited and seldom seen in Western Europe and the United States. When any of it is available, it is quickly bought up. (See Color Plate 135.)

Goldoni's pieces are primarily of sculptural form with fine internal decoration that embodies the theme—a difficult feat in itself. He received First Prize from the city of Zagreb in 1959 and the Bavarian Government gold medal for sculpture in glass in 1968. Living where he does, with limited opportunity to produce his glass sculptures, Goldoni has not had many exhibitions. His work has been shown in a number of Yugoslav cities, among them Porec, Split, Ljubljana, and Maribor, and in the following shows:

II Triennale, Zagreb, Yugoslavia 1959

Le Salon de Zagreb, 1965–69

Zagreb Museum of Arts and Crafts, one-man show, 1967

International Exhibition, Munich, 1968, 1969

301.
Raoul Goldoni, Yugoslavia. 6″. Signed
"Raoul Goldoni"

300.
Raoul Goldoni, Yugoslavia. 10¼″. Signed "R.
Goldoni"

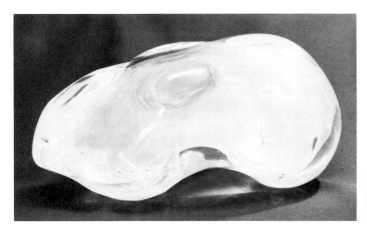

302.
Raoul Goldoni, Yugoslavia. 6″. Signed
"Raoul Goldoni, 1972, Head of a Doe"

303.
Raoul Goldoni, Yugoslavia. 12½″. Signed
"Raoul Goldoni, 1972"

BIBLIOGRAPHY

Anonymous. "Pate de Verre by Daum." *Pottery Gazette*, XCIV, no. 1108, October 1969.

Bayne, Tom. "Maurice Heaton's Laminated Panels." *Craft Horizons* XXX no. 4, August 1970.

Beard, Geoffrey. *Modern Glass*, Studio Vista Ltd., London, Dutton, 1968.

Bethell, Tom. "Joel Philip Myers" *Craft Horizons* XXIX, no. 5, September–October 1969.

Bittermann, Eleanor. "Heaton's Wizardry with Glass." *Craft Horizons*, vol XIV no. 3, May, June 1954.

Bruner, Louise. "Glass Workshop." *American Artist*, Arts and Crafts Issue, vol. 33 no. 2 issue 322, February 1969.

Burton, John. *Glass—Philosophy and Method.* Philadelphia, New York, London: Chilton Book Co., 1967.

The Corning Museum of Glass. "Glass 1959." Corning Glass Center, New York.

The Corning Museum of Glass "Census of Glass Working and Glass Decorating Schools," 1970.

Craft Horizons. American Craftsmen's Council.

Ceramics and Glass from Finland, January 1970.

D. A. "Ruth Hull and Per Lutken." *Dansk Kunsthandraerk*, 39, no. 4, 1966–67.

Erikson, Erik. "Joel Myers." *Craft Horizons*, XXVII no. 2, March–April 1967.

Ertberg, Marianne. "Ann og Goran Warff." *Dansk Kunsthandraerk*, 40, no. 1, 1967–68.

Falck, Ole. "Oiva Toikka Sculptor in Glass." *Form*, 66, no 526, no. 8, 1970.

Farrell Bill. "Pat Swenson—Boris Dudchenko." *Craft Horizons*, XXX, no. 3, May–June 1970.

Faulkner, Roy, and Ziegfield, Edwin. *Art Today.* New York: Holt Rinehart and Winston, 1969.

"Glass Review." *Czechoslovak Glass and Ceramic Magazine*, nos. 9 through 12, 1971; no. 1, 1972; no. 8, 1971.

"Glass Review." *Czechoslovak Glass and Ceramics Magazine*, Special Issue: 1969 Art in Glass.

"Glass by D. Labino, R. Marquis—J. Wayne." The American Craftsmen's Invitational Exhibition, Seattle, 1966.

Gould, Elizabeth. "Harvey Littleton." *Craft Horizons* XXVIII, no. 4, July–August 1968.

Hlava, Pavel. "Glass and Ceramics in British Design Centre." *Czechoslovak Glass Review*, XXII, no. 9, 1967.

Kampfer, Fritz, and Beyer, K. G. *Glass, A World History*. London: Studio Vista Ltd., 1966.

Labino, Dominick. "Visual Art in Glass." *Art Horizons*, Dubuque: William C. Brown Co., 1968.

Labino, Domick. "Dominick Labino Demonstrates." *Ceramic Monthly*, 15 no. 9, November 1967.

Lacey, Betty. "Contemporary Corner: Dominick Labino—Glass Artisan." *National Antiques Review*, II, no. 1, July 1970.

Libensky, Stanislav. "Paper 201," International Congress on Glass Comptes Rendus II, Bruxelles, 1965.

Littleton, Harvey K. "Artist Produced Glass: A Modern Revolution." *Glass Review*, XXIV, no. 7, 1969.

Littleton, Harvey K. *Glassblowing, A Search for Form*. New York: Van Nostrand Reinhold Co., 1971.

Lucas, John. "Erwin Eisch and His Revolutionary Glass." *Glass Review*, XXIV, no. 3, 1969.

Meisel, Alan R. "California Glass Workshop." *Craft Horizons*, XXVII, no. 5, September–October 1967.

Mankora, Blazena. "Art in Glass." *Glass Review*, XXIV, no. 11, 1969.

Mariacher, Giovanni. *I Vetri Di Murano*. Rome: Carlo Bestetti, Edizioni D'Arte Milan, 1967.

Mildwoff, Steven, and Smith, Dido. "Edris Eckhardt, Four British Schools." *Craft Horizons*, XXVIII, no. 6, November–December 1968.

Nilonen, Kertlu. *Finnesches Glas*. Helsinki: Tammi 1967.

Nordness, Lee. *Objects U.S.A.* Studio Book. New York: Viking Press, 1970.

"One Man Glass." *Country Life*, CXLV, no. 3752, January 30, 1969. Harvey Littleton, Sam Herman, R.C.A.

Penfield, Louis. "Ingebord Lundin of Orrefors." *The American Scandinavian Review*, LVII, no. 1, March 1969.

Perrot, Paul N. "Exhibitions: Toledo Glass National." *Craft Horizons* XXIX, no. 1, January–February, 1969.

Perrot, Paul N. "Robert Willson: Sculpture in Glass—An Appreciation." *Art Journal*, XXIX, no. 1, Fall 1969.

Polak, Ada. *Modern Glass*. London: Faber and Faber, 1962.

"Production at Orrefors." *Potters Gazette*, XCIV, no. 1099, January 1969.

Romare, Kristian. "Glass for the Art of Tomorrow."

Schwarzler, Gertrud. "Das Handwerk Pras Entiert Sich in Einer Galerie" [Glass by E. Eisch and Zwiesel]. *Kunst und Handwerk*, 13, no. 9, September 1969.

Slemin, Edward. "Czechoslovak Glass at the 1967 Universal Exhibition in Montreal." *Czechoslovak Glass Review*, XXII, no. 1, 1967.

Smith, Dido. "Harvey Littleton." *Craft Horizons*, XXIX, no. 3, May–June 1969.

———"Exhibition: Harvey Littleton." *Craft Horizons*, XXX, no. 6, December 1970.

Slemin, Edward. "Czechoslovak Glass at the 1967 Universal Exhibition in Montreal." *Czechoslovak Glass Review*, XXII, no. 1, 1967.

Stensman, Mailis. "Mona Morales Schildt," *Form 63*, no. 496, no. 6, 1967.

Schjodt, Liv. "Nytt Norsk Glass" [Recent Glass by Hadelands Glasswork.] *Nye Bovytt*, 28, no. 3, 1968.

Sindelar, Dusan. "New Creations in Glass by Pavel Hlava," *Glass Review* XXV, no. 6, 1970.

Schaltenbrand, Phil. Review of "Exhibition, Boris Dudchenko, Morgantown, W. Va." *Craft Horizons*, XXX, no. 5, October 1970.

Steenberg, Elisa. *Swedish Glass*. New York: Gramercy Publishing Co.

Schryver, Elka. *Glass and Crystal II*. New York: Universe Books Inc., 1964.

Smalands Museum, *Vaxjo "Glas Riket,"* Vaxjo: 1968.

Toledo Glass National II 1968.

Toledo Glass National III 1970.

Toledo Museum of Art. "Art in Glass." 1969. Text by Otto Wittman, Paul N. Perrot, Tracy Atkinson, Edgar J. Kaufmann, Jr.

Toledo Museum of Art. "Modern Glass." *Museum News*, Spring 1969. Text by Otto Wittman, John W. Keefe.

Troy, Jack. "Exhibitions: Boris Dudchenko." *Craft Horizons*, XXIX, no. 2, March–April 1968.

Treib, E. Marc. "Marvin Lipofsky—Just Doing His Glass Thing." *Craft Horizons*, XXVIII, no. 5, September–October 1968.

Turner, Helen. "Glass Design at Edinburgh College of Art." International Congress on Glass, Comptes Rendus II, Bruxelles, 1965.

Venini. "Recent Designs by Tapio Wirkkala." n.p. 1970.

Wilson, Kenneth M. "Contemporary American Studio Glassmaking." *Annales du 4 Congres des "Journées Internationales du Verre" Ravenne–Venise, 1967*. Liège.

Wonderful World of Ohio. "Labino's Glass Objects d'Art." March 1970.

Widman, Dag. "Grace and Shimmer in Glass."

MUSEUMS AND COLLECTIONS

UNITED STATES

Addison Gallery of American Art, Andover, Massachusetts
Albion College, School of Fine Arts, Albion, Michigan
American Crafts Council, New York, New York
Arizona State University, Tempe, Arizona
Arnot Art Gallery, Elmira, New York
Art Institute, Chicago, Illinois
Bennington Museum, Bennington, Vermont
John Nelson Bergstrom Art Center and Museum, Neenah, Wisconsin
Brooks Memorial Art Gallery, Memphis, Tennessee
Burpee Art Gallery, Rockford, Illinois
Butler Institute of American Art, Youngstown, Ohio
Capital University, Columbus, Ohio
The Cleveland Museum of Art, Cleveland, Ohio
The Chrysler Museum of Art, Institute of Glass, Norfolk, Virginia
College of Mount St. Joseph, Mount St. Joseph, Ohio
Columbus Gallery of Fine Arts, Columbus, Ohio
The Cooper Union Museum, New York, New York
The Corning Museum of Glass, Corning, New York
Detroit Art Institute, Detroit, Michigan
Detroit Children's Museum, Detroit, Michigan
Elvium Art Centre, Madison, Wisconsin
Flint Institute of Art, Flint, Michigan
Fowler Museum, Los Angeles, California
Henry Ford Museum, Greenfield Village, Michigan
Henry Gallery, Seattle, Washington
Hopkins Center, Dartmouth College, Hanover, New Hampshire
Illinois State University, Normal, Illinois
Indiana State University, Terre Haute, Indiana
Indianapolis Museum of Art, Indianapolis, Indiana
Ithaca College Museum of Art, Ithaca, New York
Joslyn Art Museum, Omaha, Nebraska
Krannert Art Museum, University of Illinois, Urbana, Illinois
Lowe Art Museum, University of Miami, Miami, Florida
Massillon Museum of Art, Massillon, Ohio
The Metropolitan Museum of Art, New York, New York
Miami University Alumni Building, Oxford, Ohio
Milan Historical Museum, Milan, Ohio

Mills College, Oakland, California
Milwaukee Art Center, Milwaukee, Wisconsin
Mint Museum of Art, Charlotte, North Carolina
Museum of Art, University of Michigan, Ann Arbor, Michigan
Museum of Art, University of Nebraska, Lincoln Nebraska
Museum of Art, Newark, New Jersey
The Museum of Contemporary Crafts, Museum of Modern Art, New York
Neville Public Museum, Green Bay, Wisconsin
Oakland Art Museum, Oakland, California
"Objects U.S.A.," Johnson Wax Collection, Racine, Wisconsin
Ohio University School of Fine Arts, Athens, Ohio
Oshkosh Public Museum, Oshkosh, Wisconsin
Peoria Art Museum, Lakeview Center, Peoria, Illinois
Phoenix Art Museum, Phoenix, Arizona
Sacramento State College, Sacramento, California
San Francisco Museum of Art, San Francisco, California
The Smithsonian Institution, Washington, D.C.
Tacoma Art Museum, Tacoma, Washington
The Toledo Museum of Art, Toledo, Ohio
University of Vermont, Robert Hull Fleming Museum, Burlington, Vermont
University of Wisconsin, Madison, Wisconsin
Utah State University, Salt Lake City, Utah
Western Illinois University, Macomb, Illinois
Wichita Museum of Art, Wichita, Kansas

FOREIGN

Civic Museum of Venice, Venice, Italy
Das Danische Institut, Dortmund, West Germany
Die Stadtische Gallerie, Oberhausen, West Germany
Derby Museum and Art Gallery, Derby, England
Formsammlungder Stadt, Braunschweig, West Germany
Frauenau Glass Museum, Frauenau, West Germany
Fucina Degli Angeli Gallery, Venice, Italy
Gulbenkian Museum, Lisbon, Portugal
Groningen Museum, Groningen, The Netherlands
Kunstindustrimuseet, Copenhagen, Denmark
Kunstindustrimuseet, Oslo, Norway
Kunstgewerbe Museum, Cologne, West Germany
Kunstgewerbe Museum, Zurich, Switzerland (Bellerive Museum)

Kunstmuseum, Dusseldorf, West Germany

Landes Gewerbe Museum, Stuttgart, West Germany

Landesmuseum, Oldenburg, West Germany

Landeswerbes Museum, Baden-Wurttemberg, West Germany

London County Council, London, England

Louisiana, Humlebaek, Denmark

Leicester Museum and Art Gallery, Leicester, England

Malmo Museum, Malmo, Sweden

Mexico University Museum, Mexico City, Mexico

Musée d'Art Contemporain, Skopje, Jugoslavia

Musée d'Art Moderne, Paris, France

Musée de Verre de Charleroi, Charleroi, France

Musée de Verre de Liège, Liège, Belgium

Musée des Arts Décoratifs, The Louvre, Paris, France

Museum of Applied Art, Copenhagen, Denmark

Museum of Applied Arts, Oslo, Norway

Museum Boymans–Van Beuningen, Rotterdam, The Netherlands

Museum of Glass, Novy Bor, Czechoslovakia

Museum of Glass and Jewelry, Jablonec, Czechoslovakia

Museum Haaretz, Tel Aviv, Israel

Museum fur Kunst und Gewerbe, Hamburg, West Germany

Museum des Kunsthandwerks, Leipzig, West Germany

National Museum, Stockholm, Sweden

Neue Sammlung, Munich, West Germany

National Museum of Glass, Leerdam, The Netherlands

Narodni Galerie, Prague, Czechoslovakia

Nordfjeldske Kunstindustrimuseet, Trondheim, Norway

Palais Stoclet, Brussels, Belgium

Pilkington Museum of Glass, St. Helens, Lancashire, England

Peggy Guggenheim Collection, Venice, Italy

Portsmouth Art Gallery and Museum, Portsmouth, England

Rodin Museum, Paris, France

Rohnska Konstslojdmuseet, Gothenburg, Sweden

Royal Scottish Museum, Edinburgh, Scotland

Sammlung Veste, Coburg, West Germany

Smalands Museum, Vaxjo, Sweden

Stedelijk Museum, Amsterdam, The Netherlands

Vestlandske Museum of Applied Arts, Bergen, Norway

Victoria and Albert Museum, London, England

INDEX

Page numbers in italics refer to illustrations.